"With startling finesse and unmooring insight, *Autumn Song: Essays on Absence* will recalibrate your senses to understand there actually is no such thing as void or emptiness at all. Inside perceived absence, there is invitation for seizing, reconsidering, and creating new lexicons of poetic logic. These essays are treasures, tendered by Patrice Gopo's rare gaze of lyrical precision. *Autumn Song* is an ode to the artistry of seeing oneself in a world of fast glances and forgotten histories."

—LISA FACTORA-BORCHERS, author, activist, and editor of
Dear Sister: Letters from Survivors of Sexual Violence

"This gorgeous collection of essays about home and belonging casts a spell on me, with its gentle yet sharp observations and evocative sense of place. Like an alchemist, Patrice Gopo transforms ordinary moments into reflections on stillness and process. She investigates the destruction of a historically Black neighborhood in her town and explores the complicated nature of interracial relationships. Underlying these contemplative essays is an urgency to make sense of a world that often feels chaotic and frightening. *Autumn Song: Essays on Absence* is a necessary book, one I will return to again and again."

—GEETA KOTHARI, author of *I Brake for Moose and Other Stories*

"Patrice Gopo brings a contemplative eye and heart to the small but poignant details that comprise the miracle of everyday life. Though subtitled *Essays on Absence*, *Autumn Song* displays a hopeful focus on what is present and affirming: the warmth of a grandmother's embrace, the exquisite sound of snow melting, the quiet triumph of a deer shaking itself free after being stuck in a fence. Such observations hold the frequency of the book as the pandemic lockdown shrinks the world and casts events such as the death of George Floyd into stark light. Walking through these essays with Gopo is a profound and gratifying journey."

—SOPHFRONIA SCOTT, author of *The Seeker and the Monk:*
Everyday Conversations with Thomas Merton

"Patrice Gopo deftly plunges the reader into a life that weaves the personal with the political—and spotlights patterns of beauty amid the chaotic and often racist American fabric, both past and present. Gopo's prose is vivid and gorgeous. I remembered her memories and her family long after I finished the book."

—DEVI S. LASKAR, author of *The Atlas of Red* *and Blues and Circa*

AUTUMN SONG

AMERICAN LIVES *Series editor:* Tobias Wolff

AUTUMN SONG

Essays on Absence

PATRICE GOPO

University of Nebraska Press   Lincoln

© 2023 by Patrice Gopo

Acknowledgments for the use of copyrighted
material appear on pages 167–168, which constitute
an extension of the copyright page.

All rights reserved

The University of Nebraska Press is part of a land-
grant institution with campuses and programs on the
past, present, and future homelands of the Pawnee,
Ponca, Otoe-Missouria, Omaha, Dakota, Lakota, Kaw,
Cheyenne, and Arapaho Peoples, as well as those of the
relocated Ho-Chunk, Sac and Fox, and Iowa Peoples.

Library of Congress Cataloging-in-Publication Data
Names: Gopo, Patrice, 1979– author.
Title: Autumn song: essays on absence / Patrice Gopo.
Other titles: Essays on absence
Description: Lincoln: University of Nebraska Press, [2023] |
Series: American lives | Includes bibliographical references.
Identifiers: LCCN 2022056873
ISBN 9781496235800 (paperback)
ISBN 9781496237330 (epub)
ISBN 9781496237347 (pdf)
Subjects: LCSH: Gopo, Patrice, 1979– | Jamaican American
women—North Carolina—Charlotte—Biography. |
Jamaican Americans—North Carolina—Charlotte—
Biography. | Charlotte (N.C.)—Biography. | Charlotte
(N.C.)—Social conditions—21st century. | Jamaican
Americans—Alaska—Anchorage—Biography. | Anchorage
(Alaska)—Biography. | United States—Race relations. |
Presence (Philosophy) | BISAC: BIOGRAPHY &
AUTOBIOGRAPHY / Personal Memoirs |
BIOGRAPHY & AUTOBIOGRAPHY / Cultural,
Ethnic & Regional / African American & Black
Classification: LCC F264.C4 G67 2023 | DDC
975.60092 [B]—dc23/eng/20221130
LC record available at https://lccn.loc.gov/2022056873

Designed and set in Arno Pro by L. Welch.

For my parents.
Thank you for your enduring belief in me.

And for those who build lives amid the absences.

CONTENTS

AUTUMN SONG

By Way of Explanation

The maple tree in my front yard tells the silent story of the passing seasons. The stripped branches of winter. The promising buds of spring. The thickness of summer, spine and ligaments cloaked in an endless green. On a humid September day, six months into a plague that clawed at everyone's lives in different ways, I began taking a daily photograph of this maple tree. To ensure I remembered to pause and sit and take in the view, I set the alarm on my phone. Each afternoon, the insistent chime sent me out to the porch. I'd settle into the patio furniture while the rest of my household continued using our home as an extension of both work and school.

The flourishing tree—thousands of healthy leaves the size of my curled fist—crowded much of the view during those initial weeks of preserving the slow ache of change. A look to the left or right, though, might yield neighbors walking past or a car backing out of a driveway. A mother might push a stroller. A couple of teenagers might dribble a basketball on their way to the court. Within moments, the movement exited my limited frame, and I was left with just my tree—a tree not yet ready to relinquish the abundant spread of summer. As the temperatures started to cool, some days I'd sit on the patio couch for hours just as I'd done back in the long-gone days of spring. Mid-September marked half a year since I'd last visited a friend's home or attended church or sat inside a restaurant or brushed past a stranger on the sidewalk.

The previous spring, I had begun to shape this essay collection. The terrible days comprising the early months of a pandemic that would reach further in time than anyone could then imagine. While a few of the essays in this book had existed for years—previously published or biding their time on my computer—that spring, I took stock of what I'd already written and what I'd only begun to envision. Much of the world around me seemed to slow down, and I let my thoughts slow down as well. I asked myself, "What do these essays together want to be?"

Perhaps there was something gratifying about exerting a level of control over my writing when each day served as a reminder of our lack of control over the events feeding that year. I soon saw with fresh clarity, however, that this sense of control over my writing was merely an illusion. In fact, the writing itself, the individual words, the work of my subconscious, all these elements had a say in what this book wanted to be.

The world continued out there, beyond my home and front porch. Months passing. Ice melting. River banks rising. Helpless infants becoming cooing babies. Children walking across the bridge to tweenhood. And I began to make progress on this book. In ways I struggle to name, a pandemic brought to me the sense of urgency I often need to excise an idea from my mind and put a project in motion. I could attribute this reality to various factors: the politics, the racial violence, the disparities in health care laid bare by the pandemic, the pause that inserted itself into life as my world seemed to shrink.

Looking back, none of these reasons feels quite right when taken in isolation. However, stacked together, they encompassed a more complete explanation. How fitting, then, that this unfolding book consisted of work I'd written in the past—sometimes years before—and new essays taking shape in the midst of global havoc. These essays *stacked together* encompassed a more complete reason for the existence of the separate parts. In a time of great absence and loss, a hub of absence revealed itself as the overarching theme. Absence in so many forms. Absence in dreams deferred and hopes not realized. Absence because of loss, heartache, and disappointment. Absence arising from injustice. Absence of physical places.

Absence in experiences. Absence in memory. Absence of the life we used to live. Absence of the life we long to live. Also, the literal absences within the structure of some of the essays. The reliance on the empty spaces and section breaks to speak ideas as well.

Who I am at the time of compiling the existing essays and writing new ones guides this book. Even more, though, who I once was, at the time of writing older work, also leaves a permanent fingerprint on these pages. Each essay tells the story of the particular version of me I was when I wrote those words, a snapshot of an ever-changing human being. As a result, when I look back on some of my earlier work, I have a visceral desire to rewrite parts of those essays. I want them to more closely reflect the person of now, not the person of back then. I could certainly have revised and rewritten. However, over these months, I've discovered I want to leave these essays primarily unchanged. In doing so, I allow them to serve as both an artifact from my individual history and a contribution to the artifacts forming our collective history. And what a sweet epiphany for me to recognize that my choice to leave these essays by and large alone creates another interaction with the theme of absence. While I am writing these words now, the person who narrates portions of this book is—in some ways—no longer here. She is absent. (To stretch this truth even wider, I also acknowledge that by the time this book of essays reaches a reader, aspects of the person I am now, the person typing this introduction today, aspects of this person will no longer be part of me).

Ultimately, to preserve those older essays as they were is to preserve the memory of that part of myself. Yes, I have made a few slight alterations here or there. However, I have generally not gone back and reworked older essays to reflect the new wisdom, ideas, and perspectives now present. Rather, I offer a fluctuating view on absence and loss and discovering the stories within. Despite implementing these boundaries, I can imagine how I might have reshaped a couple of essays. Even in the case of more recent work, there's often another thought or reflection or bit of information

I want to add. A truth of this creative life is that we complete the writing, but we continue with the living. So, for some of the essays, I have included a short author's note (see page 169). I offer a glimpse at what has transpired since I wrote that essay, or I consider the impact the living has had on how I look back on the writing.

Each season bears the marks of change. Autumn, however, publicly smears that story on a canvas. As I sat on my front porch, I knew what would soon arrive for my maple tree, the radiance of color, the flimsy leaves fluttering in the wind, the crumbling crinkle beneath a passerby's feet. In those first weeks, though, imperceptible shifts moved through the roots and trunk, forging ahead to the tips of branches. Shifts that would soon twirl the proximity of summer into the true signs of fall. All the while, the discrete forms of absence in the essays twisted together. Perhaps the accumulation of these absences spoke to the continual absence we all experience in the face of a changing life. Those early pandemic months, a time drowning in the unknown, seemed to heighten this truth we live out each day but often fail to notice. Absence may not be absence as we often think. Absence can be a form of presence emerging, telling a tale that invites us to consider life from another perspective. The presence of absences and empty spaces in the essays reveals the flashes of glory around us and in our lives. In a world marred with brokenness, these glimmers speak to the possibility of grieving losses, healing heartache, and allowing ourselves to change.

Six weeks after I started preserving a daily image of the tree, the first dash of red outlined a handful of leaves. Then, a few weeks later, all the brilliance and decay descended and reached near completion in approximately ten days. Overnight, it seemed, or more accurately over three nights, the leaves deepened to crimson and scarlet and finally a hint of wine. In technical terms, the tree ceased producing chlorophyll in preparation for winter. The disappearance of the chlorophyll revealed the pigment always there. To my eye, though, heaven poured out a can of paint, gushing over the leaves, saturating them in the picture I'd long been craving. Autumn's distinct aroma, slightly sweet and full of earth, flavored each inhale. Over those ten days of transforming colors and falling foliage, the absence of summer green gave way to the absence of leaves. Together, these absences welcomed the presence of the next season.

By late November, I sat on my patio, capturing the image of a bare maple, this living thing gone dormant, hunkering down for the coming winter. The vacant branches gave me a direct view of the street, my neighbor's house, the world beyond my front yard.

DWELLING

Blueberry Season

My youngest daughter tilts her head up at me as I buckle her into her car seat. She asks, "Can we go pick blueberries?"

I think, *There is no blueberry season in Charlotte.*

Her request comes just a week or two after our strawberry-picking season. She recalls how I took her and her older sister to a farm flush with rows of low strawberry bushes. She tangled her fingers in the leaves and thin branches and found fruit the color of rubies. We later gathered around the kitchen table and lingered over strawberries rinsed in a colander. We discarded stems and mashed fresh fruit in our mouths. On the heels of the late-spring strawberry season and prior to the midsummer descent of peach season and well before the tangy tart of apple season—when we leave Charlotte and drive two hours to the mountains for the day and pull ripe apples from a lush and giving orchard—my daughter says she wants blueberries.

"Too hot," I tell her as I consider everything I've ever heard about blueberries, how they need cooler northern climates and mild summers. Charlotte is too hot in the summer for blueberries—and for me too if I consider the weight of the summer rays, the thick humidity that clenches the air, and the sweat beading around my hairline and dripping down my back. The air conditioner inside my home calls to me like a pied piper. I respond without protest.

"We need to go to Alaska," I say to my girl. "We need to travel to a place with a real winter." I think of Anchorage, where I come from, the city I left twenty years ago.

"Will we drive?" she asks me from the back seat as we join the traffic on familiar Charlotte roads and pass storefronts I've seen each day for six and a half years.

"Yes," I tell her and catch her eye in the rearview mirror. "We'll drive to Alaska, and we'll pick blueberries." Waves of my imagination roll over me, and I plan how we'll drive days home to Alaska and fill our plastic pails with mounds of violet fruit. For the few moments I have the attention of a preschooler, together she and I dream. I plant a story of a long, winding road trip across the country, through Canada, and into Alaska, all in search of berries I think we can't pick here in Charlotte.

This is my seventh summer in Charlotte. Six and a half years now in a city I thought might be a passing-through home. But my husband, my girls, and I, we are still here—beginning our seventh summer. Seven. The days of creation, the colors in a rainbow, the number of completion. Is seven also the number of years that signifies Charlotte is now the foundation for my family's life?

Many summers ago, when I was a child in Alaska, my parents, my sister, and I collected pails of low-bush blueberries first from the slope of a mountain and later from the valley close by. We hiked into the hills near Anchorage and plucked the jewels that clung near tiny leaves, handfuls plopping in the bucket and at least as many more bursting in my mouth.

"Blueberry jam," my mother declared, and she used a recipe a friend with extensive Alaskan roots had given our transplanted family. A recipe to boil the berries, stir in cups of granulated sugar, and add other ingredients I can't recall. We set a row of jelly jars across the kitchen countertop and inhaled the fragrance of syrupy sweet. My mother poured the deep violet jam into each jar, and my sister and I helped tighten the lids. We used black permanent markers to write down the date and lined the pantry with jars of homemade blueberry jam. For the next few months whenever we wanted jam with slices of toast or paired with peanut butter sandwiches—perhaps all the way until that spring—we drew a jar from the pantry, unscrewed the lid, and remembered the slope of a mountain and the taste of fresh blueberries.

My mother is planning to leave my hometown of Anchorage

and move to my Charlotte neighborhood. My father left when my parents' marriage ended years ago, but my mother has stayed through forty-three winters of navigating ice-caked roads. And forty-three summers in mild weather offering just enough respite from the snow. My mother wants to be near her granddaughters. She wants them to come spend weekends with her and visit her on sweltering summer days. My mother has never spent a full summer in Charlotte, but soon she will. Sometimes in the midst of a Charlotte summer, when the heat bears down with an even greater intensity, I think of my Anchorage mountains. I think of temperatures ten, twenty, thirty degrees cooler. I think of days perfect for the flourishing of wild Alaskan blueberries—and overcast heavens spilling forth the crisp comfort of home.

*

On the phone, on an ordinary day this summer, my mother tells me that she will put her house on the market in autumn, that she will pack her possessions, leave Alaska, and create a home down the road from me in Charlotte. The distance between my family and her will compress to mere streets, to a number of houses between, no longer the stuff of a thousand miles thrice over. I know these happenings usher in a time of the beauty of generations entwined, but I taste a slight bitterness in my mouth and the words slow.

"Wow. It's sad," I say when I think of her home sold and the way I'll no longer be able to tell people my mother lives in Alaska.

My mother echoes my words. "It is sad," she replies and there is a long pause in our conversation.

My daughters play down the road at a summer camp, running around a playground, sucking on ice popsicles, and living the lazy days as I once did far away in Anchorage. I stand in my garage, preparing to pick them up from a day of fun. My mother is coming to us. Next year she may be preparing to pick up her granddaughters from a day at camp, bring them back to her house, and watch them create imaginary games at the edge of the woods in her new backyard. As I drive the couple of miles down the road, I recall my mother's back deck and the mountains the color of blueberries in the distance and the way we were living like Alaska would always be home. I have gorged myself on the reality of a life rooted somewhere. Even as I've left Alaska, my mother's presence there allows me to taste these ties to a familiar place. And with my mother's words, with the few months left, I find the flavor I long to hold beginning to evaporate into nothing but memories.

I pull into the camp parking lot and pause a moment to glance at the height of the surrounding trees and the expanse of the manicured lawn. The months ahead will bring laughter and long hugs, shared meals and creation of the future—something new to alleviate the weight of the loss of my childhood home pressing against my chest but perhaps never dissipating.

*

Days after I speak with my mother, my family and I spend a Saturday a few hours from Charlotte. We pass the afternoon on a farm on the outskirts of Chapel Hill, sipping cold drinks, seated on stools in an open-air tea house void of walls, windows, and doors. In each direction we turn, we spy plants and shrubs used in this eco-friendly business. Lavender and jasmine. Hyssop and hibiscus too. A couple of hummingbirds hover near a clump of leaves, their wings a blur. Bees buzz around, and I envision raw honey sold in canning jars. When I purchase my glass of lavender lemonade, I spot a sign that reads, PICK BLUEBERRIES HERE.

Blueberries? Here on this plot of land lit with summer heat, never knowing the chill of real winter cold? The girls and I wander past picnic benches and a makeshift playground to rows and rows and rows of blueberry bushes. We pluck the berries and begin to fill a quart-size crate to brimming, working steadily in the shade of a few trees, stripping each bush of its bounty. My girls want to move farther down the row, but I keep us in the shade, the brute sun sure to transform the fun of berry picking into absolute drudgery. After we fill our quart and before we wander back to the tea house, replete with spinning fans and cups of ice water, I take a photo of my youngest holding the cardboard container of berries. We stand not on the slope of a mountain, but here on this flat patch of ground beneath a grove of trees.

"We didn't have to drive all the way to Alaska," I tell my daughter as she poses with her blueish-purple treasure. Here, just a few hours from our home, the blueberries grow in quantity enough to satiate and satisfy.

Winter's Breakup

In Charlotte, where winter brings no guarantee of snow, small children press their palms together, close their eyes so tight they see waves of color, and plead with God to unzip heaven. And last night God answered their prayers, pouring a fine dusting across the hard ground. This morning the radio says, "No school." Twitter commands, "Stay off the roads."

After my young daughters step into seldom-used boots and pull fuzzy hats over the tips of their ears, I open the front door to the sound of melting snow. Sunlight brightens our path, and rivulets of water gush down the road. Gray concrete peeks through our trail of footprints. Tiny icicles clank against the ground, succumbing to the same warm rays beating my brow. Tomorrow, I will stand on this bare sidewalk, absent the melting song that declares the cold can't remain.

In my childhood home, we referred to today's symphony as "breakup." Breakup in Anchorage was a thing of weeks, maybe stretching beyond a month. A whole season. First winter. Then breakup. Finally spring. After months of snow and ice, breakup reminded us that winter could not prevail. That spring would always swallow death. Drops of water plunking against frozen ice. Tiny rivers in search of street gutters. Frozen fangs released from roofs, shattering against porches and decks. My rubber boots—breakup boots, we called them—pounding puddles, splashing slush.

Now, in my front yard, thin blades of dead grass poke through the snow. The girls lean back on the white lawn, thick tights and fleece pants shielding them from the damp. Flapping their limbs, their bodies add earthly angels to the world.

"Listen," I say. "Do you hear the snow melting?"

"Listen," I say again.

Can they know the music? Can their ears discern those sounds in a world where snow leaves in a day? Tomorrow we will stare at yards returned to winter's norm, at our world carrying on in muted colors. Then on a Saturday in the near future, we will awaken to the hum of lawn mowers and the telling fragrance of freshly cut grass. Without realizing it, we will step into a season that splashes pinks, purples, and vibrant greens on flowers and buds and lawns.

But what of the waiting, what of the longing for an end to the gray? What of a season that reminds us of what we leave, but hints at what will come? The in-between time when we start to believe for another year that winter will pass. When we muster hope that the spring we remember will come again.

Standing in the driveway, I watch the girls tumble around the yard, puffed out with coats, weighted down by pastel boots. They lean toward the ground and run mittened hands across the snow. We walk to the sidewalk, a mixture of feathery white and patches of wet concrete. Around me the air sings, and the shape of my mouth mirrors my daughters' smiles. The girls remove their mittens and run fingertips across chunks of ice while I languish in the dripping, the cracking against the ground, the music of today's breakup.

Feel the ice, I think as I watch my daughters. *Feel the melting ice.* With both her hands, my oldest breaks a frozen gem into smaller stones. She presses a piece against her cheeks. My youngest takes another to her lips. And I imagine what I hear today, I will hear tomorrow, and the next day. Until one bright morning, a bird will sing amid fresh buds pushing through the branches of a tree.

That Autumn

On the last official day of summer, a Wednesday in late September, I woke to an ashen dawn. Overnight, the weather had shifted from sweltering heat to highs predicted only in the 70s. Local and national news covered the same story. The previous afternoon, a fifteen-minute drive from my home in Charlotte, a police officer had shot and killed Keith Lamont Scott, a black man.

The day had already begun out of the ordinary. My three-year-old daughter was home from preschool, having gone to bed the night before with a fever. Keeping her home meant I'd miss my weekly prayer group at church. So, while my daughter slept longer than usual, I spent the morning reading about Scott's death—protests late into the night, crowds that turned violent, an interstate shut down. I considered my sick girl and released a breath of gratitude for a fever and the excuse to remain home. I thought of my friends in prayer group and imagined their white faces turned toward me, the one black person, full of questions. "Why, Patrice? Why the violence? Why the riots?" I had my hunches, but I didn't actually know. What I wanted to avoid was feeling forced into being a spokesperson for my race. I knew all I would be thinking was, "Again?" and "Will this ever end?"

Our nation had witnessed a tumultuous summer of police shootings of black men—Alton Sterling in Baton Rouge, Philando Castile in St. Paul, and—just days before—Terence Crutcher in Tulsa—as well as civilian shootings of police officers. That day, a hazy gray blocked any hope of sunlight and crippled the present with the weight of an overcast sky.

In the days that followed Keith Scott's death in September 2016, large groups marched through uptown, carrying signs with phrases like "Resistance is Beautiful" and "Justice 4 Keith Lamont Scott." The city declared a state of emergency, implemented a curfew, and called in the national guard. I found myself wondering if the events unfolding in this city—a place I had only recently started to think of as home—were about so much more than one police shooting of one black man and the question of whether he was armed. As debate unfolded, I returned to my research of a long-gone black neighborhood that once occupied a portion of Charlotte's city center. Several days before, I'd started digging into the history of Brooklyn. Now I studied the past against the city's backdrop of tension. Perhaps this place I happened to be investigating held answers to my speculations. I made my way to Charlotte's main library, blocks away from where, at other hours of the day, masses gathered and marched through the city streets.

A few years after I'd moved to Charlotte, I'd first learned about the old Brooklyn neighborhood during the Community Building Initiative's bus tour about the city's lesser-known history. We pulled out of Little Rock AME Zion church's parking lot and turned right on McDowell Street. We lumbered past government buildings and the county courthouse and turned right again onto Martin Luther King Jr. Boulevard. Here, local historian Tom Hanchett's voice boomed with facts, speaking of stores, houses, churches, and schools that once lined these streets.

"We're now in the heart of Brooklyn," he said. I looked through the window at the couple of commercial towers, the squat government buildings, the aquatic center set back from the street. I searched for a remnant of the thriving black community that once occupied this space. Barber shops and dentist's offices. A high school and more than a handful of churches. Hanchett spoke about urban renewal, the federal government's mid–twentieth century efforts to—as it claimed at the time—clean up blighted urban areas. From my public-policy studies years before, I knew that, across the country, those "blighted" neighborhoods targeted for destruction were mainly black communities. If I'd stepped off the bus at that moment, I would have heard nothing but a few cars rushing past. No voices or greetings, no music or heels tapping against pavement. A typical story, I thought that morning, as I considered other communities urban renewal had leveled. My new city had a story to match so many others. Hanchett mentioned a plaque that commemorated what once existed on the land, but the bus rumbled past before I could spot it.

After Keith Scott's death, my thoughts toggled between present and past. How does this city's story connect with the crowds chanting at night in uptown? Maybe tucked within faded documents and old city plans lay the reasons behind the so-called riots, evidence found in old maps with black neighborhoods outlined in red and the construction of new highways that ripped these communities apart. I thought I could prove, at least to myself, that an uprising stems from the accumulation of every injustice perpetrated and every dream quashed.

On the second or third day of the protests, I sat on my patio, and my daughter ran across the front lawn in a light drizzle. A smear of sunshine worked through the clouds, and the air was sharp with the scent of cut grass. My daughter stopped mid-spin and turned to face my direction. She lifted her hand and waved.

While I watched her ordinary antics, I spoke with a white friend who'd called and said he wanted to check on us. I understood and appreciated his concern. He recognized the distance between the effect of the city's disruption on black and white people. "Are you all OK?" my friend asked. His was a question not about physical health and well-being but something more elusive: How are you coping emotionally?

"I'm not OK. We're not OK," I said with a clipped honesty. "Not OK" lacked the gravity of what stirred within me. A thesaurus of options later settled into my thoughts: terrible, gutted, angry, terrified, frustrated—none of which I conveyed to him.

Instead, I added, "None of us in this country is OK." Even if he didn't realize it, even if his insides didn't bubble with the emotional intensity those living in black bodies experienced, he wasn't immune to the impact of recent days. Maybe I thought of entire neighborhoods destroyed. Perhaps I considered how Charlotte had once been a model for school desegregation and had, in many ways, returned to separate and certainly not equal.[1] Maybe I paused to consider Charlotte's lack of upward mobility out of poverty.[2] I'm sure I thought of the protesters and their words of resistance, reverberating through the night. The history of racism in our country breaks us all. How could any of us breathing this air ever be OK?

I wasn't sure if my response startled my friend or not, or if a simple "We're fine" might have been better. I reveled in the truth of my words, though, and allowed the silence to hang across the phone line.

Political upheavals in the 1890s—among the white elite, poor white people, and black people—ultimately created Brooklyn. In a bid to hold power, wealthy white people pushed a rhetoric of white supremacy that discouraged poor white people from allying politically with black people. White Southerners enforced the Jim Crow racial caste system with a heavy, brutal hand.

White landlords built rental housing for black people in several specific pockets of the city, including Second Ward. Over time, the city prevented black businesses from accessing "white" areas of town. The grocers, barbers, cobblers, undertakers, and other business owners located primarily in Second Ward. As the years passed, black Charlotteans built a robust community within the broader city.[3] (No one knows who first called this place Brooklyn, but the name probably pays homage to the New York City borough, annexed around the same time.)

I learned this information primarily while reading Hanchett's *Sorting Out the New South City: Race, Class, and Urban Development in Charlotte, 1875–1975*.[4] Old newspaper articles provided additional facts about how the city presented the urban renewal project. "We have a file all about Brooklyn," one librarian told me. She handed me a worn manila envelope stuffed with articles that dated back to the mid-twentieth century. The clippings were thin and brittle in my fingers, and I unfolded the yellow paper with caution. The headlines proclaimed the word "slum" again and again and again: "Business Booms Where a Slum Once Festered."[5] "Slum Razing Project Approved By Council."[6] "First Slum Project Nearing Completion."[7]

"That place they tore down," another librarian said, a short woman with brown hair that fell just below her pale face. "They just tore it down," she repeated. She shook her head at the unseen "they," the "they" from long ago. But how could we have expected a different outcome given the characterization of that community as only a slum?

One morning in those days after Keith Scott's death, I left my house while the early hours remained soft and still beneath a cape of darkness. That morning, after a night of peaceful protests and marches in other parts of the city, I stood at the lip of my road. I looked down the sidewalk in my predominantly black neighborhood to where soon I would pass cul-de-sacs and white picket fences.

In those days and weeks following Keith Scott's death and the deaths of too many others, the nation once again argued about implicit bias. The preconceived ideas created in generations past about the dangers of black men. Bias against black boys in preschool classrooms. Bias against black students revealed in expulsion rates. Bias against black people in hiring practices. Bias against black men in the criminal justice system. Bias everywhere.

What I perceived in the next few hours—during my morning walk and, later, when I drove my daughters to school—is that my neighbors embraced a camaraderie born of crisis. We waved longer than normal and shared generous but wry smiles of understanding. It was as if, on that gray and drizzly day, we allowed our collective cry to ricochet among our homes and daily lives. My neighbor loaded his laptop bag into his car. He waved from the middle of the driveway, and I returned the gesture. I let my eyes lock with his for a moment, and I willed him to understand that I saw him.

A short list of places the city destroyed or displaced as it demolished Brooklyn: Myers Street Elementary School, Second Ward High School, the Phillis Wheatley branch of the YWCA, the original McCrorey YMCA, Taylor's Modern Barber Shop, East First Street, South Long Street, Pearl and Boundary, Hill and Vance. The United House of Prayer for All People, Friendship Baptist Church, Brooklyn Presbyterian, East Stonewall AME Zion, the Church of God, Williams Tabernacle, New Emmanuel Congregational, St. Paul Baptist, Grace AME Zion, Bethel AME Zion, McKissick's Shoe Shop, the Savoy Theater, Queen City Pharmacy, Alexander's Funeral Home, Hall's Meat Market, Mutt Culp's Shoe Shine Parlor, and Jack's Pool Room. Hortense McKnight's beauty shop, which I imagine smelled of hot combs used to straighten coiled hair.[8] The street where a child learned to balance on a bicycle. The tree where a pair of lovesick teenagers etched their initials into ancient bark, the front room where a baby learned to walk. The sidewalks children skipped down after school.

In his 2014 essay "The Case for Reparations," Ta-Nehisi Coates writes, "It is common today to become misty-eyed about the old black ghetto, where doctors and lawyers lived next door to meatpackers and steelworkers."[9] And I realize I'm susceptible to that gauzy view. I envision places where people cared for and supported one another, whether shoe shiner or business owner, and the sweet days before new highways knifed through black communities, splitting them apart, concentrating poverty, and relegating black people to the shadows of cities.

Coates goes on to say, "This segregationist nostalgia . . . ignores the fact that the old ghetto was premised on denying black people privileges enjoyed by white Americans."[10] Here I see the root of why I succumb to romanticizing Brooklyn—the very nostalgia Coates condemns. How could people choose to raze Brooklyn and then forget?

Charlotte couched the destruction of Brooklyn in a narrative about access to better housing and safer living for black residents. The mayor used a sledgehammer to bash in the first building.[11] None of the old articles I'd read at the library mentioned how city leaders ignored Brooklyn's declining condition as they funneled resources into white neighborhoods.

Ultimately, the rise of a glossy city center eclipsed the unfulfilled promises of replacement housing, the insufficient funds given to relocate businesses, and the terrorism carried out by white communities when potential black neighbors came too close. Much of the displaced population would move to the West Side. Half a century later, lack of opportunity in many of these communities would contribute to Charlotte ranking dead last among American cities in economic mobility.[12]

There's no question that Brooklyn was the product of segregation. Still, Brooklyn matters because black Americans in Charlotte were able to build a thriving place to live in the midst of injustice. Even more, Brooklyn matters because Brooklyn was someone's home—a home destroyed without permission or fair compensation. I want to honor this place for what it was, what it represented, and what it meant to people.

In 1973, toward the end of urban renewal and years after former Brooklyn resident Maggie Stinson lost her home and neighborhood, the *Charlotte Observer* quoted her as saying, "I sure loved it over there cause it was my home."[13]

I studied the history of Brooklyn, learned about the United House of Prayer for All People's annual parade, and read about beauty shops and barbers. In two or three lines of an article, I discovered that a predominantly white church had purchased land and built on what once was part of Brooklyn.[14]

I searched for anything church members might have said about the destruction of Brooklyn and its many black churches—about how, intentionally or not, it made space for a white one. Efforts to unearth that footnote in history produced little except the sense that the church's presence in Second Ward is a result of urban renewal, not the cause. This line of inquiry helped me see, though, that I probably wanted to blame someone or something—but who? Gone are the people who dismantled Brooklyn, the city council members who approved the project, the reporters who saw Brooklyn as a slum and little more, and the government agency that designated black neighborhoods high risks for mortgage loans, leaving them vulnerable to the whims of urban renewal and highway expansion.

So on a Sunday morning in late autumn, more than a month after Keith Scott's death, I visited that church built over old Brooklyn. I sat in the pews, smiled at the people around me, and recognized what once was here. After the service, I walked along the neighboring blocks in the cool October air. At the intersection, I crossed over MLK Boulevard, turned right, and stopped in front of the Metro School, which uses the old Second Ward High School gymnasium. A cluster of black-and-white photographs surrounded by frames of mosaic glass hang as a memorial to Brooklyn. The street was washed in silence, void of cars or pedestrians on the sidewalk. Not even a bird fluttered by, pausing at the edge of a roof. Half a block later, I encountered a plaque—the same one I'd missed all those years ago on that bus:

Second Ward School
1923–1969
Site of the first public high school for Blacks
   in Charlotte-Mecklenburg

I continued down the street and turned onto another block. At Marshall Park, with its ponds and fountain splashing into a stone basin, I stood on the withering grass, in the shadows of sycamore trees shedding their autumn leaves, and existed on another continuum. Just weeks ago—not decades ago—crowds had gathered here. Protesters stood with other souls and remembered a man recently dead and so many other men gone too. "No justice, no peace," they cried as they walked in unison past the courthouse and county jail. "Black lives matter," they chanted with handwritten signs hoisted high, stepping across the very ground where black lives had once lived. They marched for today and yesterday. They marched to remember Keith Scott's life. And I think, without even realizing it, they marched for a lost Brooklyn, a place they never knew.

The June 5, 1977, *Observer* published a photograph of a man named Vernon Sawyer, who, as Charlotte's Urban Redevelopment Commission director, oversaw Brooklyn's demolition. He stares out over what was once Brooklyn. A few buildings tower in the distance. Tidy city blocks run parallel and perpendicular through the frame. Government buildings. Commercial property. A sprawling park. The caption under the photo reads, "Vernon Sawyer Looks Out On Brooklyn Today."[15] Four years earlier, Sawyer had reflected on the transformed city. "There isn't any more Brooklyn. We ought to stop calling it that. Brooklyn is gone."[16]

He's correct. Not a ghost of Brooklyn remains. Sawyer takes in the clean, sleek lines, a testimony to what man can both create and erase.

That day I'd visited the church built on old Brooklyn, I'd sat in a pew and stared up at the stained glass window at the front of the sanctuary. Morning rays pierced the colorful panels of translucent glass, and their brilliance lured my gaze. When I turned from the sun, a remnant of direct light mottled my vision with streaks, lines, and speckles of black and bronze. I closed my eyes tight to help my pupils recover then opened them once more. No longer focused only on what lay ahead, I found that I could see the broader world, free from all that had distorted my sight.

Between Mountains and Water

This is a splinter of time ever familiar to me, the final hour of a flight to Anchorage. Sleeping passengers beginning to wake. Others shuffling down the aisle one last time. A few returning items to the overhead compartments. The seemingly endless mountain range beyond the tiny windows, awe-inducing peaks topped with a syrup of brilliant snow.

A flight attendant pauses by our row. She leans toward my daughters, busy with cleaning up crayons and card games in preparation for arrival. "Are you visiting or going home?"

"Going home," my older daughter responds. The answer tilts my girl's face from grin to broad smile, the toothy, full-eyed kind steeped in mystical anticipation. Mine almost matches hers. Home. She's never lived in Anchorage. This is her fourth visit in her nine years of life. Yes, she's tasted king salmon fresh from the Gulf of Alaska. She's donned heavy boots. She's plucked a stalk of fireweed flooded with pink flowers. But there is no constellation of everyday memories shining with snow forts in the front yard or day hikes to a glacier.

My daughter's response makes me want to hug her. "I grew up in Anchorage," I say, clarifying what perhaps matters little to the flight attendant. "We don't live there, but it's where I grew up."

"Oh, so visitors then," she states, moving farther down the aisle, having categorized us to her liking. *No*, I whisper. This is not a visit. This is a homecoming.

Anchorage is constrained by its own natural boundaries. The east rises into the Chugach Mountains, and the west dips into Cook Inlet. Between mountains and water, a city thrives. As a black daughter of this city, I once believed that Anchorage was too narrow for me to truly live. I thought the landscape did not contain enough space for my story. I strained against these boundaries even as I enjoyed expansive summer days and snow tubing down packed winter trails. My imagination carried me to sprawling metropolises, bustling sidewalks, and an abundance of faces like mine. I left for college, searching for those places, eventually settling in North Carolina. Over two decades later, I'm now a cliché. Boundaries that once confined have become generous limbs welcoming a daughter home. I crave the embrace.

My first book is a tribute to that journey: a collection of essays about growing up as a black girl in Alaska and searching for my way out into the larger world. I return to celebrate this book with my oldest community. Fittingly, its cover is adorned with blue ridges and a smear of sun. My daughters and I will stay for a mere week, a week that will hold readings and public conversations, an evening with a book club and a day of workshops at my old high school. As the plane dips, I settle into the rhythm of a journey I've flown countless times. I turn toward the window and look past my younger daughter to the clouds gathered in gentle tufts. I am going home.

We arrive in mid-autumn when the chilly air is pregnant with the possibility of the first real snow. My older daughter, prone to occasional coughing fits, inhales deeply and breathes with ease. When I turn the faucet to cold, ice water bellows from the tap and quenches my thirst. For just a moment, as I pause at a traffic light, the reality of the city's backdrop startles me. A length of plum ridges and valleys seemingly suspended from a clear sky. Then the panoramic view blends into my unconscious, letting me take it for granted as one is wont to do in their home. One morning, I rise for an early walk. A dense darkness clutches the day, and a foggy mist dampens my coat and face. My girls and I are staying with a family friend, and I begin walking through this neighborhood I've walked in many times before. "Moose, moose," a stranger's voice calls. "There's a moose in my front yard." Up the block, the scruffy outline of the large beast comes into focus, illuminated by a porch light.

"Thank you," I call in response to the stranger's warning. I take several steps back, turn around, and carry on my way.

My birthplace never seems grounded in my most recent memory. Instead, she's grounded in the accumulation of memories I formed over my first eighteen years. Despite altered traffic patterns and new shopping plazas, I struggle to remake this place in my mind. Once, years after I left Alaska, on the horizon, the gray of Cook Inlet encroached on mud flats and approached a line of evergreen trees. The scent of frigid ocean twisted through the air. Across the foamy surf and steel-colored waves, crinkly clouds obscured a range of peaks. Then. Then I remembered. I remembered I was walking in my Charlotte neighborhood. Not Anchorage. As my eyelids opened and closed and opened again, the mountains became clouds. The water transformed into a thin strip of sky. I wanted to weep at my mental mistake. For some time afterward, I longed for what I had left, the landscapes, the water, the signs that tell me where I'm from.

What happens when you no longer live in your home, but your first instinct to make sense of the tangible occurs through the lens of that place? Then, a horizon might appear as an inlet the color of flint. Anchorage is not just as I remember her, though. New roads run through areas once forested, and double-laned pavement has replaced gravel streets. Development and glossy new buildings alter the expanding cityscape. When I visit my old high school, a student raises her hand and asks, "What's changed since you went to school here?" She sits near a boy from Sudan and another from Thailand.

"So much," I say. I stand before a classroom comprised mostly of students of color. The demographics have shifted. The structure of the school differs too. The hallways, they are larger now. The classrooms boast more light. A multiyear remodel created common areas with circular tables. This is not my school even as it is my school. I wonder what my story would be had I attended this version of the school twenty years ago. Would I still have heeded that call to explore? When I look out the windows, my eyes settle on what rises beyond. I finish by adding, "Those mountains, though, they remain unchanged."

A few nights later, at another friend's house, my girls borrow mittens and run around in the backyard with her children. We gather for dinner followed by warm raspberry-rhubarb pie. I savor every tangy bite. As our forks scrape the last of the fuchsia filling, I tell the story of the flight attendant on the plane. This is how I answer questions about what it's like being back. "There should be another word that means more than visitor," I say. "Even if I don't live here, this will always be my home."

*

During the late summers and early autumns of childhood, when leaves began to fall beneath birch trees and the air cooled, the salmon returned to spawn near my home. Once silver, they were now bright red with age, weary bodies finding their birthplace. They swam upstream from Cook Inlet, through slender waterways beneath the Seward Highway, arriving back in a comforting marsh. My parents, my sister, and I would walk down the boardwalk built over that marsh and hang our heads and arms over the railing. We would watch as scores of salmon flicked their fins against the familiar currents, piercing a trail home.

A few summers ago, I leaned over my kitchen counter and wrote tally marks on the back of a used envelope. One for each year in Anchorage and one for each year away. Eighteen tally marks—almost—for my childhood. A tally mark for the year before I married. A tally mark for the two summers I spent in my twenties living at home. Twenty marks for years in Alaska. Eighteen marks for years away. With gratitude, I noted that I'd spent most of my life in Alaska. Now I am nearing forty, and soon, this will no longer be true.

Years, maybe decades, in the future, when I am older than I am now, I will not question whether I have lived more or less of my life in Anchorage. With plenty of silver hair and a slower gait, I will return to this place I call home. I will sit at a table in my favorite restaurant and feast on an open-faced crab sandwich and steaming slabs of sourdough bread. I will drive down the Old Seward Highway or Northern Lights Boulevard and take in the sight of fresh buildings and trendy coffee shops amid occasional storefronts that hint at the past. Then I will head to the water, sit on a boulder near the mud flats, and watch the tide rolling back out to sea. I will turn my head to what lies behind me in the distance. And I will see those peaks, stare at them, and soak in their permanence.

At the beginning of our week, my girls and I arrived in the early afternoon. For the final portion of our flight, we cruised above the ridges buried beneath snow. "Look," I told my daughters, pointing out the window to the glory of sunlight reflecting off peaks. Now, at the end of the week, we depart in the middle of the night. A red-eye flight to Seattle and a return trip to Charlotte. As the plane ascends, leaving Anchorage behind, I find I straddle a space between my original home and a place becoming another home. This time no flight attendant asks, "Were you visiting or are you leaving home?" But I need not be constrained by limitations in vocabulary. If asked, I would answer, "I am anchored." Not a visitor, but anchored to this place. Beyond the window, it's impossible to make out the landscape cloaked in a raven black. I pull my travel blanket around me and take comfort in knowing mountains and water remain, even as I go.

Dispatches from a Walking Life

I wake to a pewter hue of no-longer night and not-quite first light, to the intermittent roar of car engines, to the cadenced breath of my husband Nyasha close by, to the steady bird chatter calling for another morning. I grab shorts and a T-shirt. Nyasha turns in the bed and scoots over to my side. I whisper into the darkness, "Back soon." Quiet steps carry me down the stairs, my slumbering daughters across the hall. In the garage, I pull on my shoes, the outer edges worn as my soles each day press against pavement. Although unseen, I have carved an indelible path through my Charlotte neighborhood. Each day my body rounds road bends I've long known, the route a labyrinth that will always return me to where I began. On the best of mornings, just as I start my ascent up the hill, I tilt my head upward. To walk alone is to answer the summons of a swollen sunrise.

In the beginning, walking was about my body, my shape, the jeans I couldn't button, the way I looked in the mirror with extra pounds appearing in my butt. Walking was about the slacks that squeezed my thighs when I sat all day at work. In those days, I was working my first post-college job in upstate New York and struggling to figure out a balance between daily lunches out with coworkers and the new stagnant nature of my life. Weight loss became a riddle to solve, and I surmised walking might hold an answer.

Each morning. Two miles to the lake's beach. Two miles home. Within weeks, my body began to shrink into my clothes. Nearly two decades later, I continue to walk.

A snake carcass interrupts my walking path. Burgundy, bent into an S. A passing car left it partially flattened, the concrete dulling to red. I hold my phone above the remains, and the camera preserves the image—as if what I see is otherworldly. It is a snake, but does a carcass convey other meaning? Does such a sight on my path serve as a veil for something more?

In the aftermath of George Floyd's murder, protests are catching fire, reaching across the country, spreading around the world. *These are holy flames*, a white friend wrote me. Holy flames. Streets pulse with protesters. Storms of "Black Lives Matter" and "No more. No more. No more" shake cities and wake psyches. Perhaps the carcass is telling me something is dying, and what has been can be no more. More likely, though, it is just a dead snake, in the midst of summer, smashed on the road.

My mother has cautioned me from rising too early, walking in the near dark, walking with only an occasional streetlight, walking when no one else is on the road. My mother worries something will happen. Still, I follow my patterns. Turn left. Turn left again. Or turn right. Turn right again.

"Stay safe," my neighbor has called to me when our walking paths have intersected. Over the years, we've passed each other more times than we can count.

"I will," I've replied. "You do the same." A certain casualness embodies this just-past-dawn exchange as if we control how the day might unfold, the jolt of the unexpected and unanticipated pushed far away. And I will carry out the motions of staying safe, keeping to sidewalks and removed from the road, pausing at crosswalks and looking right, then left, then right again. Small acts that offer no guarantee.

Ahmaud Arbery jogged through a suburban neighborhood, and two white men murdered him in the strong sun of midday. Months passed before law enforcement made arrests.

Each morning I walk not just as a person. I walk as a black woman. From my country's inception and 150 years prior, this adjective has been a reason, an excuse, a justification, a classification, a declaration.

During my first year of walking in upstate New York, a car of guys yelled at me, "Fifty dollars for a blow job!" Their shouts startled me from my mental meanderings. Their raucous laughter burned my ears as they sped away.

Later, I thought, *Because they're creeps. Because they're idiots. Because I'm a woman. Because I'm black. Because I'm a black woman. Because I'm opposite them.*

Clarity matters little. Now they've forgotten a moment that attempted to remove something of my humanity—but called into question their own.

A dog and owner walk toward me, and I cross the street. I offer a smile and a wave. In the past, a neighbor mentioned that I should carry a long stick. "Just in case," she said. In case the dog defies their owner's friendly claims. In case the animal breaks from its leash. On rare occasion, an unleashed dog roams the streets. Ambling. Meandering. Pausing. Sniffing the ground. I adjust my loop, walking another way.

Bird-watcher Christian Cooper asked a white woman to obey a sign and leash her dog. She refused. She said she would call the police and tell them, "There's an African American man threatening my life." All because she didn't like being asked to use a leash. Later, she blamed her actions on her "bad day." Her bad day. Christian Cooper's possible nightmare.

Not long ago I noticed a rabbit's bloodied and broken body left dead by a passing car.

"Do rabbits have funerals?" one of my daughters asked later when she heard the story.

"His family probably doesn't know yet that he isn't coming home," Nyasha replied.

My throat constricted and my lungs sighed and my fingers paused and my eyes lost sight of the kitchen scene. What turned my vision fuzzy, what gave me pause, what startled me was not a dead rabbit, but only this, "His family doesn't know yet that he isn't coming home." For eight minutes a police officer had held his knee to George Floyd's neck. When had his family realized he wasn't coming home?

Halfway through chapter 3 of the Book of Ecclesiastes reads, "Whatever is has already been, and what will be has been before." To walk the same route each day is to embark on a journey already known.

A woman stands in her driveway and says, "You do your walk. You inspire." Her neighbor dressed in gym clothes follows with, "I'm right behind you." And as I begin to ascend the hill, a car rolls to a stop, the driver calling out, "Keep working out! You have the strongest legs in the community."

Sometimes when I'm out at the grocery store or pumping gas, a stranger approaches me. "You're the woman who walks. I see you every day." Within a moment, I'm acquainted with a neighbor. They recognize me as someone who passes by their house while they drive to work or sit in their living room looking out the front window. Until they greet me, though, they remain a mystery. They know me, but I do not know them. Me walking out in the open. Them nearly unseen in their cars and homes.

To my left I see the home that shares our street number. Similar address. Different street name. Every few weeks, their mail arrives at our house. The first time this happened, Christmas lights framed homes and the glow of sparkling trees illuminated front windows. That time of year, all packages are soaked in joy, delight, and expectation. "Let's return this," I said to Nyasha. "Not tonight," he answered. Not that night when we might be unknown black people ringing doorbells of anxious strangers. Not that night with moonlight camouflaged behind cloud coverage and no guarantee of who might answer the front door. Not that night when all we'd wanted to do was be neighbors and human beings thinking of other human beings. "Tomorrow," Nyasha said.

The next morning, I detoured from my pattern, leaving the package on their front stoop. Then I returned to my route and walked away.

On a chilly winter day, I found a toddler. She stood barefoot by a mailbox, clothed in thin pajamas. My footsteps slowed to a stop. Closed doors. An empty street. A stranger's child now my responsibility.

Any child can turn a lock, I reasoned. *But if I call the police now, I'll change this family's life.* A brown baby removed from her mother. I did not need to wonder what to do next—to pick up the little girl and hold her to my hip, to knock on doors until I found her home. I knew to do all of this because I am a living body. For some time, I wandered up and down the street with a growing group of neighbors until we discovered a half-open front door. A bleary-eyed, confused mother appeared as we called into the home. That morning, I returned a child to her family.

The house at the corner of the neighborhood has a peach tree. I only realized one day when I stepped over fruit rotting on the ground, the near-sickly sweet of fermentation surprising me. Part of the tree leaned across the fence and over the sidewalk. Pale orange spheres dropped from the branches, and I spied more than a few nestled in the leaves. A peach tree, I marveled. A peach tree here in my neighborhood, growing, blossoming in another's backyard. Unharvested fruit dropping to the street. This was a sight I hadn't before seen in this community. In the countless miles I've walked through this neighborhood, this was the first time I'd noticed a peach tree, mature and for several years—likely—in plain view.

The wind is with me. The current brushing my arms. The motion rattling branches and shifting clouds and rustling welcome flags in front yards. A burst of fabric softener wafts past my nose. Without me seeing, the wind tells me who is drying their clothes. The wind—today a breeze, tomorrow a whistling gust—accompanies me, but I do not pay attention. I forget the invisible walking with me. The signs, though, appear in what I hear and smell and feel.

Once Nyasha told me he'd heard a story on the radio about tortoise season. In people's backyards, at fence boundaries, near the divide between grass and trees. There, they made their appearances. "You shouldn't move them," he added, since a tortoise lives his whole life within the boundary of a square mile. Move a tortoise, and he'll spend the rest of his life trying to return home.

When I left my home this morning, when I reached the end of the driveway, I made a decision. Right or left? A walk to the front of my neighborhood or a journey back? In the nearly ten years I've lived here, I've watched new homes manifest from the dust. Long stretches of earth the color of sunbaked clay transformed to cul-de-sacs and additions to the community maze. I have watched apricot sunrises and stepped around puddles and waved at neighbors I see each morning and let quiet fall over me in a soundless and wordless prayer. I have listened to the cries of my thoughts and attempted to solve puzzles without solutions and pondered dreams as yet unborn. And sometimes in those early hours, as splinters of sunlight streak the horizon and the scent of morning dew rises into the air, I have seen off to the side the waxing or waning moon before it disappeared behind the blinding rays.

Always, always, though, my walk returns me to my home.

Not today but other days beads of heavy rain slap the pavement, and my open garage reveals a slick, shiny road. Frothy water zigs and zags to the gutter. The rush of cool air leaves me trembling, umbrella in hand, as I stare at thin lines falling from the atmosphere. A day dressed in the weave of melancholy. On such days, often I snap open the umbrella, persisting despite the weather. Some mornings, though, perhaps the sky mourns and the clouds weep. Before I even begin, I close the garage and return to my bed.

Each death that comes is a death to mourn. The names trickle from my mouth and the list expands each day. Breonna. Atatiana. Eric. Michael. Sandra. Terrence. Their lives were not meant to symbolize anything more than the life of a soul wrapped in a body. Flesh. Bones. Tissue. Muscles. A body's breath taken and skin left to rest against grime and sediment. A life removed from Earth. And with the snuffing of spirit, a person shifts from living to symbol. The names, their humanity, stolen and their memory welded to a just cause. They no longer walk this earth, even as each morning I rise and walk again and the next day again and the next day again. Is this erasure? George Floyd the individual disappears, transformed to a symbol. We were never meant to be symbols. We were meant to live. We were meant to breathe.

Today I will return to my home, and I may sit for a few minutes on my front porch. *What swept by me this morning?* I will think. Pools of cloud coverage will moderate the heat of the day. *What swept by me?* And in that moment of idleness, I will try to summon the specifics of what I saw in the light of morning. The houses blending one to the next. The daylight running alongside shadows. A rabbit hopping across a yard. A cardinal perched on the upper branch of a tree. *Was that today?* I may wonder. *Was that today?* Or was that the grave of yesterday or the grave of last week? For one yesterday scalded my arms. Another yesterday the heat left an outline of my tank top on my skin. Yesterday the sweat pooled at my forehead and along my temple. But this yesterday, I looked up to a ceiling of clouds graying the sky. And yesterday I walked beneath the shelter of an umbrella. Yesterday I saw my breath extend like steam each time I exhaled. Yesterday I curled my fingers inside my mittens, fisting knuckles to palms to keep them warm. Yesterday I wore shorts and a tank top. Yesterday I wore jogging pants and my long, heavy coat. Yesterday a trio of eagles danced beyond the tree line. Yesterday a dozen deer skipped across the street. Yesterday a pair of rabbits disappeared in the woods. Yesterday the wind loosened amber leaves from our maple tree. Yesterday became a tithe of what fades and returns. Yesterday I walked almost four miles in the searing sun, in the fog, in the mist, in the rain, in the cold. Yesterday became the day before yesterday and the day before yesterday's yesterday. Yesterday piled upon yesterday into yesteryear.

What swept by me this morning? I will think as I trace my steps as if under some hypnotic spell. In the summer humidity folding into present reality, in the endless, intermittent chorus, pitch, and chime of singing birds, in the ordinary activity of cars driving out of the neighborhood and people opening their front doors, I will feel what I feel each day if I pause long enough. The common miracle of breathing in and breathing out, of occupying the category of living.

I walk to nowhere. Today, like every other day, is one loop followed the next day by another. Loop upon loop growing into an endless spiral of loops. One day people will say things about my life. I adored my husband. I spent afternoons on my front porch. I loved ice cream. Perhaps, most of all, people will say I walked. I walked and I walked and I walked. Nearly four miles almost every day. Enough steps that by year's end, I have walked well over twelve hundred miles. In a year I could have walked past Austin, Texas. I could have walked past Indonesia in ten years. Except each step returns me to where I began. I've been living in this neighborhood watching everything turn green, morph into autumn, fall off trees, bud, and repeat. Up the block and around the corner, circling cul-de-sacs and waving at neighbors. I remain in the same place. My mind spins daydreams floating out of my body, floating everywhere and nowhere. In a decade, I have walked twelve thousand miles in my neighborhood, and I remain standing here, returning to myself again and again, each day different and the same.

Birds chirp balanced on street signs. Highway traffic groans beyond a dense wall of trees. My laces flap against my shoes. The whispers remain the same. To the pavement and the staring rabbits and rising dawn, my footsteps fold into every other act of morning. And the seemingly silent symphony cries, *Yes, the day is new, but the path is ancient.*

LIVING

Stones of Remembrance

Two weeks into a new decade, I turn the pages of my planner to February and find the 29th. An extra day on the calendar. An additional Saturday this time, appended to the shortest month of the year. I envision a party at our home complete with a spread of treats and games and paper for constructing origami leap frogs. Later, my thoughts amble toward extending invitations to friends to join Nyasha, our daughters, and me for a group hike to a cluster of boulders where children—and adults too—can leap around the formations. The ideas grow, buoyant and alive.

My memory returns me to a leap day almost twelve years ago. I sat on the floor, leaning against a wall, my dying phone plugged into an outlet. That February 29th, Nyasha began *us* from across the ocean and over the phone line, him in Cape Town, me in Anchorage. What he said pulled back the façade on months of conversation and connection masked as friendship. *We are more than friends*, he said—not in those exact words but as close in meaning as I can recall. The conversation divided our relationship into before and after, the event converging the lines of our individual lives into a shared path.

Begin with me, Nyasha said that day. Not an actual marriage proposal, but I hung up the phone with a certain confidence that the one on the other side of the line, the one on the other side of the world, I would marry that one. On a day designed to collect the extra twenty-four hours accumulated across four years, my little world shifted.

As we gather in the kitchen preparing lunch, the girls ask their father, "What do you like that Mommy wears?" I look over at Nyasha, curious at how he'll respond. In his eyes, I often feel as if every outfit I pull from my closet shines. Nyasha's compliments about my clothes always delight me even if I haven't given a lot of thought to the question my daughters asked. His compliments do not arrive every day, and I sometimes solicit them. "You look really nice," he'll say in passing as I examine my reflection in the full-length mirror or we climb in the car for church. As he is not one for adding much specificity by identifying a particular garment or color, his generalities communicate something more than appearance. Maybe closer to the realm of "I love you."

Nyasha pauses for a moment, looking off to the side. My clothes must swirl through his mind, the colors and cuts coming into focus along with the seasons for certain outfits. "Mommy's dresses," he says, and my expression becomes a full-faced grin. Across our marriage, he has dropped countless compliments about what I sometimes wear as my spring, summer, and early autumn uniforms. Years ago, perhaps prior to marriage, I realized that dresses can serve the perfect double duty: comfortable and easy, yet also evoking a particular style that leaves me smiling at myself in the mirror.

"And she's had some of these dresses for years," he adds. He goes on to mention a blue dress with wide straps and white polka dots that I wore often when we were first married. Nyasha describes the dress, and I grow silent, searching in my mind for what I know is no longer there. The place in the closet that dress once occupied is now empty. My mental mind map draws a branch with a large sack of clothes destined for the thrift store—now long gone. Not because I didn't love the dress but because I rarely wore it. It had somehow fallen off my regular dress rotation, replaced with newer clothes.

The next morning, I rummage through smooth rayons and crushed cottons, searching for blue fabric with white polka dots. Of course, I come up with nothing except old memories. The dress discarded, as I already know, in a flurry of cleaning out my wardrobe and simplifying my life. When Nyasha wakes I will tell him the dress found a new home through a thrift store donation. He will pat my shoulder and tell me not to worry. It's not a big deal, he'll say. It's only a dress. And I'll agree that it's only a dress. Since the beginning of our marriage, though, he liked the dress and I didn't realize how much and I gave that dress away. Maybe his view of the dress became a symbol returning to bloom with the onset of spring. Year in and year out. He would be here. I would be here as well.

There is imperfection in the number of days it takes the earth to revolve around the sun. One turn of the earth's axis equals one day. In 365.2422 days, the earth completes an entire solar revolution.[1] Close to perfection and yet not quite. As a result, those who arrange time and set time, these people who imagine themselves with authority over time, they say that every four years we must slip an extra day into the calendar. Every four years, we correct our course or else, at some future date, the snow will fall in the summer. The Egyptians first thought of this idea. Julius Caesar created the original system with his Julian calendar. Pope Gregory XIII added a hint more precision, implementing the calendar we use now.[2] Regardless of the presence of leap day, though, the earth would continue to rotate around the sun, yielding spring, summer, autumn, and winter. However, in the absence of leap day, our months migrate from the correct seasons.

Patterns appear. Or we create patterns. Nestled there, we believe our flourishing will blossom. Leap day matters because we want the consistency of the coldest temperatures in the winter months and planting at springtime. Perhaps the loss of the dress mattered to me because its presence would have suggested the consistency of a marriage building toward longevity.

I keep stones of remembrance. Artifacts that remind me of who Nyasha and I were and who we've always been to one another. A scrapbook that includes wedding photographs and the invitations I tirelessly designed and made. A watercolor portrait above our fireplace a dear friend painted of Nyasha and me. The emails Nyasha and I exchanged in the months I lived in Anchorage and he lived in Cape Town. I printed those email exchanges and paid Kinko's to bind the ream and a half of paper with a fat plastic coil. I presented the epistles—for that is what Nyasha and I called those lengthy electronic letters back and forth, back and forth—to Nyasha on our wedding day.

Shortly after Nyasha and I married and I moved to Cape Town, a friend started telling me that if our marriage didn't work I could just come home. Her statement troubled me even as I stared at the wedding photographs taken on a Jamaican beach and cupboards filled with mismatched coffee mugs, slowly building a just-married home. At first, I thought my friend was perhaps jealous or thoughtless or a little of both. I sought others for advice. "Why do you think she keeps saying that? Why do you think she mentions divorce again and again?" People shrugged. People told me they didn't know. One day I wrote her an email. *Your words bother me.* Hadn't she attended the wedding and witnessed the vows and watched the abundant folds of fabric and walked through waves cresting the sand? Hadn't the scent of ocean water wafted beneath her nose? I'd never mentioned strife. What did she see that I didn't know?

"I'm just saying what I would want to hear," my friend explained. "There would be no shame in something not working and then deciding you wanted to leave Cape Town and come home." Now I see what my friend already knew. Amid the newlywed glow, it is possible that a couple's distinct paths may never converge into a united one.

Leap day works because of the discrepancy between the length of a day on Earth and the number of days needed for our planet to revolve around the sun. The imperfect pressed into near perfection. A planet that spins on itself, returning to its daily starting point every twenty-four hours. And that same planet uses 365 of these rotations plus just about six hours to spin around the sun. It might sound almost flawless, and yet this reality is far from exact. One could imagine a full revolution taking 365 days and one hour, giving rise to a leap day once every twenty-four years. Or 365 days and thirty minutes, giving rise to a leap day once every forty-eight years. The desire to track time and pin human planning to the solar system necessitates leap day. There is much we cannot control, but with leap day we succumb to the illusion that the planetary world can be fully tamed.

Before I married Nyasha, an acquaintance told me about the long-distance relationship she and her husband shared prior to their marriage. She mentioned letters he wrote her, letters she saved. By the time I met her, she'd been married in the realm of several decades. Perhaps longer. During a rocky season in their relationship, she found her husband's letters at the back of her closet, reread each and every one, and remembered why she loved the person she had married. She told me that the old letters saved their marriage. When I told her the date Nyasha and I had chosen for our wedding, she smiled. She said, "That's our anniversary."

Nyasha and I return to our epistles without any set interval. The book of letters sits in a box, resting in our closet. Occasionally, one of us pulls the box from the top shelf and opens the pages, leaking the scent of computer paper into the room. The girls may be there, looking for dates that connect with their story. "Hey, that's my birthday," one says. "And here's my birthday," the other adds. Nyasha and I flip through the emails, and I remember my long-ago self seated for hours at the computer, composing just the right response.

Most days I think nothing of the over four hundred and fifty thousand words exchanged between two people growing to love each other despite a vast distance. I just move through the ordinary acts of living the life we have made together. Sometimes, though, sometimes my arms find purpose in that walk-in closet. I might stand there and reach for the stack of books I'll give the girls when they are older. Or I pull from the top shelf the bag of hair beads I keep in that space as well. In such moments, the bound book's red cover peeks out from a corner of my line of sight. My face brightens, and my body overflows with the familiar feeling of how Nyasha and I began. And when I next see my husband, I offer that smile to him. Or I may clasp his palm.

Another friend tells me she hasn't found marriage to be hard. As she says this, I recall a time, years ago, when I sat with a group of near strangers in the basement of a church. Somewhere the Bible-study discussion veered, and one woman mentioned the general challenges of marriage, the difficulties that arise as two people agree to join their lives together. This meshing of hearts may produce searing flames of frustration along with the tender desire to sit close to one another. I thought then, and I'm sure I quipped, "Marriage hasn't been hard for me. Sometimes I wonder what I'm doing wrong because it hasn't been hard the way everyone says."

I often think that I could probably tally the number of times Nyasha and I have engaged in an actual argument. We rarely fight over the mundane or the immense, who should vacuum the living room, who should pursue their dream. Nyasha and I have passed through the years in a comfortable understanding of one another littered with sprinklings of conflict. But those conflicts stung and once festered in some way. Take the morning three months after the birth of our first child when I crushed Nyasha with, "It's always me. I pick out her clothes. I decide when she goes to bed. It's always me." My words became a tornado bashing his shoulders into defeat. Despite such memories, that day in the church basement, I thought, *These years have not been hard years.* And now I know of the multitude of ways in which I lived within the cartography of my own flawed imagination. Inaccuracies hid reality. As I read about leap day, I discover that even this extra day of compensation is an imperfect solution. I read that leap years, in fact, do not happen every four years as I've always thought. Exceptions exist to this rule of four.

Every four years except in a centennial year that cannot be divided evenly by four hundred.[3] Think 1700, 1800, and 1900 versus 1600 and 2000. Think 2100, a year Nyasha and I will not live to see. Think that no solution and no way of being yields perfection without some hint of problems.

In the years since that church basement, I have realized that to fight or not to fight, to disagree or not to disagree, to reach impasses or not, to hold unmet expectations or not, these events do not, by default, determine the presence of marital harmony or discord. *Marriage*, I thought, as my friend spoke of the ease she and her husband experienced in their marriage—*marriage*, I thought to myself, *is hard because each person places themself in imperfect alignment with another human being.* In the absence of perfection, anything else holds flaws. Keeping seasons in sync with our calendar holds challenges. Keeping two people in sync with one another holds challenges as well.

In the early years of our marriage, Nyasha and I waltzed through a daily exchange of money, him home in the waning evening light, sweat soaking his wrinkled shirt, and his hands turning out his trouser pockets, pouring out loose change from the day—the bronze and silver and gold coins, fifty-cent, ten-cent, one-rand, and the best, the ones I would dig through the metal tin for the next day, those coveted five-rand coins I stuffed in my pockets, ready to buy myself ice cream cones, chicken for the evening dinner, and an excuse to engage with strangers in my new Cape Town life. We lived our early years of marriage in that way, him making, me spending, him giving, me taking.

Our movements and steps became the actions of two human beings inching their way into a collective journey. Those were beginning days, when we were off balance, self-correcting, and searching for some sort of equilibrium. Were we to live it all again, perhaps I would want to alter the particular pattern we adopted. Perhaps I would not.

In a way, the new decade returned Nyasha and me to where we once existed, the continuum that long ago stitched together our lives, the days in which I collected coins discarded from Nyasha's work trousers. Ten years prior, on the first day of 2010, Nyasha and I preserved notes and objects in a used gift box: one of his old work shirts, the outfit our daughter wore when she came home from the hospital, letters we wrote to each other to read in ten years' time, the menu from the Thai restaurant where we dined that New Year's Eve. I sealed the box with tape and wrote in black marker:

Gopo Family Time Capsule 1 January 2010
to be opened 1 January 2020

Between 2010 and 2020, the box disappeared and reappeared, disappeared and reappeared again, traveling from Cape Town to Anchorage to Charlotte. And when the new decade arrived, we unpacked the time capsule packaged ten years prior. We cut through the clear tape and stood at the kitchen counter, revealing what we hadn't seen in so long. I stood with my people, Nyasha, the girls—two of them now, their excited cries buzzing in my ears. One by one we revealed the relics that once told the story of our lives. The menu. The letters. The shirt. The outfit giving off the mild scent of once-used baby detergent. We sifted through what we'd stored. Nyasha and I read notes we'd written to each other and the notes we wrote to a baby who we knew back then would be on the brink of leaving childhood. I searched the letters for something prophetic clinging to the words. What I found, though, was the almost imperceptible fever of homesickness—not for a particular place but for a particular time. A sort of longing lingered as I remembered our flat in Cape Town, the trio of windows that overlooked the communal garden below, the metal tin where I searched for coins, the drying rack I placed on our tiny balcony. I dropped my arm over my younger daughter's shoulder. Of course, I wanted her—and countless other aspects of what these years have brought. But I also wanted to pinch a part of all that we left behind in time.

Perhaps to encounter one's past and remember who two people once were, this becomes the extra leap day infused in a marriage. The very act draws one person back toward the other. The nostalgia points to the reason we wake with one another each morning, the reason I regret the dress tossed in the giveaway pile, the reason I watch rainstorms on the front porch with Nyasha. Here, I also discover a sliver of me misses the time from long ago.

On February 29th, we do not host a party or go hiking with friends. I never suggested these plans to Nyasha, and I tell myself this is because he is an introvert. He'd wish for a quiet day. The truth, though, is the twining together of two individuals, each incorporating aspects of the other person. Over the years, Nyasha's introversion has nurtured something new in me. I relish quiet moments and silent walks and a day spent with my books as much as I enjoy dinner out with friends. In this decade plus, Nyasha's reflective ways and patterns of silence have drawn me from the shiny thrill of dazzling conversations and deep laughs. So, this February 29th, we spend an afternoon by a lake, skipping stones across giant ripples. I sit back on a roomy, flat rock and watch Nyasha and our younger daughter crouch, side by side, on a boulder jutting into the water. He holds a stone. She holds a stone. Nyasha demonstrates the way to toss so when it hits the water, it bounces once and then again. But each of her stones *plunks* before sliding below the surface. I watch her try to mimic her father's stance, but her *plunk* never quite matches his *plink, plink*. "Never mind," I say to her. "Never mind. You're doing great." Then I say what I can only say today, "Next leap day you will know just exactly what to do." Next leap day—as in four years in the future. On the lakeshore, both girls find shells that remind me of the sea, the color slightly worn by the water current. They gather their shells, and Nyasha joins me on the rock. We sit close, but our bodies don't touch. Our arms rest in our laps.

I lean over and whisper, "Ice cream." He nods back at me, and there in the woods we plan out the closing act for this day that marks both our beginning and our world's moment of realignment. There are reasons for this Saturday, ancient Egyptian insights, a Julian calendar, and—much later—a Gregorian calendar as well. An earth that takes six hours longer than 365 days to rotate around the sun. There are attempts at precision, attempts at keeping growing seasons in line with our human tracking of time. There are all these explanations. But I do not claim a definitive understanding as to the whys and hows of alignment. Together, Nyasha and I watch the lake ripples and our daughters collecting shells along the shore. I look to where, moments ago, he crouched low and showed a child how to make a stone leap across water.

Raised to Life

In the nightmare I find my toddler face up in a shallow pool. Her vacant eyes haunt me. Her clothes balloon with water. I lean over, yank her out, and hold her lifeless body in my arms. I wake, open-mouthed, to the din of absolute silence.

Now alert in the night, I can split dream from reality. I know my daughter sleeps close by. But I see those marble eyes. The limp body. The spreading circle of damp on my imagined clothes.

*

I am eleven years old, and my pastor dunks me into a baptistery filled with water. *Raised to walk in new life,* I hear when pulled to the surface. A large towel greets me as I exit, my clothes heavy on my limbs, a puddle forming at my feet. Beneath the comfort of the fabric, my skin feels the cool air, and my body begins to shake.

In the future words gush with great force. Well-intentioned opinions flood my mind and make my lungs burn for breath. I hear instructions, taught as tenets of this faith, about being submissive, respectful, and the keeper of the home. A role, I'm told, assigned from the time the Tigris and Euphrates rushed through Eden.

There are things I will come to regret. The way I shrank myself, the way I silenced my voice, the way I believed that idea to be truth. But I will not regret that moment of immersion.

*

I gave birth to my daughter in a tub of warm water. She slid from the sac of fluid within me to the birthing pool surrounding me. Below where I crouched and pushed, she could have remained there for seconds, minutes, maybe more, her body attached to a pulsating cord.

But the midwife's hands sank below the surface, cupped my girl's wrinkled body, and guided the fresh baby to her mother. Thin skin pressed against my wet chest as I waited for a scream that never came. Just the flutter of a heartbeat and a soft mew.

"The gentle birth," the midwife said while she drained the tub. "Water babies don't really cry."

*

Sometimes I daydream about my girl far in the future when she is big and grown. She stands on the bank of a great river or walks barefoot beside the ocean's lapping tongues. Her blinking eyes stare into a blurry distance beyond the range of my imagination.

And I think how, around her, words can rise. How jagged twists on a faith I have handed her may one day creep close and soak her shoes, her clothes, her being. But my daughter, I dream she floats in the river current, breathes with the ocean's waves. Her strong arms cut through walls of water in a way even her mother never knew.

Why did I believe the church's patriarchal teachings for such a long time? Because I didn't know there existed a way to stop and yet remain.

*

In the bright of morning, after the time for nightmares is over, I hear my toddler's waking cries. Later we walk past a fountain. Her squeals prod me to stare with her at slim arcs of water splashing into the pool below. I loosen my grip on her hand and watch her touch the slight spray of what she has known since her beginning.

I Think My Grandmother Has Forgotten

On the two-hour drive to my sister's house, I tell my older daughter about the time my grandmother slaughtered my pet chicken. Nyasha's hands hold the steering wheel, and my toddler sleeps with her cheek pressed against her car seat. But my six-year-old focuses on the story about the woman we will soon see sitting on the couch in my sister's home.

"A family friend gave your auntie and me a chicken," I tell my daughter. I then explain how one day, when my sister and I were away at school, my grandmother walked with her machete to the makeshift coop in our backyard. She grabbed the chicken and chopped off its head.

"Then Gong Gong cooked it for dinner," my daughter adds, using the same name my grandmother called her own grandmother long ago in rural Jamaica. My daughter has heard the story before, and she doesn't flinch at the chicken's beheading.

"Yes, Gong Gong made a curry out of it." I chuckle at the thought of my grandmother's no-nonsense behavior. Her life in rural Jamaica happened decades before I was born, far from the suburban American neighborhood where I grew up. I imagine she struggled to believe that a chicken was supposed to be a pet. I can also imagine that an activity like slaughtering a chicken must be similar to riding a bicycle. Even if decades have passed since one last killed an animal, a person can't forget the way the hand holds the feathered body. Or the way the opposite hand grasps the smooth wooden handle of the machete.

Except a person can forget, and I think my grandmother has forgotten.

*

When I was about eight and my grandmother a bit past sixty, she called her daughter-in-law—my mother—and said she was going to retire and come help my parents care for my sister and me. She left New York City, her home since leaving Jamaica, and came to Anchorage, Alaska, the place my parents had settled after my father's time in the military. With two working parents in our home, my grandmother shouldered many duties, easing the strains of managing life. She walked my sister and me to the bus stop and was there when we came home in the afternoon. What I remember most, though, is the way her hands spent their days in a whirlwind of motion: holding the handle of a hot iron as she pressed my father's work shirts, twirling a wooden spoon while she stirred substances in great cast iron pots, hovering over a vegetable garden plucking weeds. Even in rest, she sat with a word search puzzle in her lap, a pencil in her hand, making quick circles around the found words.

The color of my grandmother's hands is brown like mine but with a tint of sunlight. These days she sits with those golden hands folded in her lap, no longer twitching or looking for something to make the fingers move. Now she doesn't long for pulling weeds in a garden. And if my daughter had a chicken, her Gong Gong wouldn't remember the steps to transform the pet into a fragrant curry dinner.

Why does the brain do this? When the brain decides to forget, to carve out gaps in memory, why does it leave the hands idle?

Once upon a time my grandmother came to help my parents care for their children. Now the years have passed and the roles have changed. My grandmother lives with my sister, who helps her get ready in the morning, reminds her to take her medicine, and offers her more water to drink. From time to time, my sister even wipes away my grandmother's tears when she remembers how much she forgets.

My older daughter was in preschool when my grandmother came to live with my sister. In those early months my sister and I talked about the similarities in our caretaking roles. The overlap as we both cajoled others to eat or go bathe or both.

As time has passed, though, I have watched my daughter develop greater independence and shoulder her own responsibilities. And my sister has watched the eager help my grandmother's hands once offered diminish. These days, my grandmother sinks into the couch while the sounds of old television shows fill the living room and transport her to the past.

*

At the end of our drive, my sister answers my daughters' pounding fists, and my girls leap through the front door. A dance of hugs ensues, and my grandmother rises from her spot on the couch. Her smile extends across her face, and I know my sister will tell me later that Grandma had a good day because we came to visit.

"TC," my grandmother says, standing in front of me with her hands pressed against my shoulders. She stares at me, her eyes lively. I smile at her use of my old nickname. She stares a moment longer before adding, "It's been so long since I last saw you. So long." Her hands drop from my shoulders, and her arms wrap around my waist, bringing me into a hug.

"Yes, Grandma, it's been so long," I say to her just like I said last month.

In the kitchen, my older daughter says to her aunt, "Gong Gong asks the same questions again and again." I hear silence and know my sister pauses, taking a moment to gather her words. I'm glad my family lives close enough that we can make this trip often. There is a sweet joy that comes when I watch my grandmother's face brighten at the appearance of my daughters. Even more I think of the lessons of life, love, and family my daughters discover during these times.

"She asks the same thing over and over," my daughter says again.

"Yes," my sister explains. "Gong Gong's brain is sick. She has a hard time remembering things."

My daughter accepts this answer. Later, when we all are leaving a museum and walking down the sidewalk to the parking lot, my daughter calls, "Wait, Mommy. Don't forget Gong Gong." I turn and see my grandmother lagging behind.

While there are no guarantees about what the mind will do in the future, today I don't forget. I tell my daughter about my grandmother's hands, which were once in constant motion. I pour over my daughter stories my grandmother no longer remembers. Perhaps one day my grandchild will speak to her daughter the stories I no longer remember.

Now, though, I stare up the sidewalk at the generation ahead of me and the generation behind. "I'm coming, Gong Gong," my daughter says. She runs back and glides her smooth fingers into her great-grandmother's wrinkled hand. I watch them, linked together by laced palms, walking toward the rest of their family.

When the *Challenger* Exploded

When the *Challenger* exploded on a late-January morning in 1986,
you were not in a classroom. You were not bunched with other
children on a schoolroom rug, your eyes focused on a television
screen. You did not "ooh" as the space shuttle lifted from the ground.
You did not gasp when seventy-three seconds later that same shuttle
exploded, trails of smoke spreading into the shape of a Y.[1] Now
you're several years past thirty-seven, past social studies teacher
Christa McAuliffe's age when she perished with the crew. Back then,
though, you spent your days in elementary school. However, unlike
many of your contemporaries, you never watched the demise. The
Challenger exploded at 11:39 a.m. Eastern Time in Cape Canaveral,
Florida. Across the country millions of children sat in their classrooms watching what NASA had arranged for them to see in real
time. But you lived in Anchorage, Alaska, another time zone. At
7:39 a.m., you sat in your mother's blue Subaru as she drove across
town to the school where she worked and you attended. Not a
classroom, but a car.

Memory, though, memory can be a fickle thing. Sometimes
to recall the *Challenger* is to see yourself seated cross-legged on
the carpet in the corner of your second-grade classroom. Details
surface. The television set rolled into the room. A shuttle rising
through the sky and clouds, moving toward space. The smoke.
The flames. The fearsome reality. Imagination flips into inaccuracy.
This make-believe sequence teeters far from reality. You were in
first grade that year, in a classroom gone from your memory. The
Challenger exploded before you arrived at school. You did not watch
that moment as it happened. You can't even recall the recap that

evening when your parents turned on the nightly news. When you think of the *Challenger*, really think about it, you recall the "very special" episode of *Punky Brewster*—a children's sitcom. The title character ran into her foster father's arms. "Henry," she cried, "the space shuttle exploded." And as an adult when you follow that memory's trail, you discover the episode aired almost a month and a half after the disaster.[2]

Further research tells you only a quarter of the country's five-to-eight-year-olds witnessed the *Challenger*'s destruction. Less than half of nine-to-thirteen-year-olds tuned in.[3] Not the number of children you had imagined. Perhaps enough, though, for a cohort to form a corporate memory, a memory in which you visualize yourself as standing on the fringe. The way you think about the many moments after the moment is an interlocking collective memory where people rehash where they were and how they found out. Within an hour of the explosion, 85 percent of the country knew what had just occurred.[4] Mental images of watching live blended into clips from the news, creating the container a child—or an adult—might use to hold that day.

*

At your first post-college job as an engineer, you learn the real reasons for the *Challenger* disaster.[5] Temperatures below freezing. Broken seals. Lack of testing on the O-rings. You discover how the failure has become a case study. A sadness, perhaps melancholy, creeps into you and your coworkers as you all consider what happened. Later, you also discover when the *Challenger* exploded, it didn't really explode. A broken fuel tank set in motion events that released liquid oxygen and hydrogen. The resulting ball of flames looked like an explosion.[6] Without the fuel tank, the *Challenger* plummeted into the Atlantic Ocean. An explosion imposter. You also wonder if perhaps you are an imposter, a generational imposter, a person of a certain age in your country who didn't witness the event volumes of others seem to recall. And if you are an imposter, somehow wedging yourself into this generation, then you question if this is the place where you belong. Isn't belonging about connecting with the common denominators, the typical experiences, the public events? The whisper of reason rises fierce and fast, dismissing your abstract theorizing, reminding you that generations form from the simple logistics of being born. By virtue of birth, you are firmly planted. What else then, what else might it mean to belong?

Years later, at a writing conference, a speaker asks the audience to list a societal event taking place within one's personal history. Your thoughts wander for a moment until swerving toward the *Challenger*. Not because of what you know. Because of what you don't know. Along with the room, you explore memories present and memories absent. What you remember: Punky Brewster and her tears, the way the show made you imagine circles of elementary school students seated on a carpet, talking through their trauma. What you also remember: the discovery later in life about the seals. What you don't remember: teachers fidgeting with televisions on wheeled carts, six- and seven-year-olds sitting at their desks or gathered on the floor, the shuttle exploding into a flurry of debris, first graders sobbing, reports on the 6:00 p.m. news.

Some children sobbed while you joined with the ones sitting in traffic on the way to school. Not that you wished to see what those children saw, you think, your pen scrawling quick, messy notes. Not that you actually wanted the stark realization to capture your classroom, the piercing reality of viewing death. At the writing conference, a stranger's words startle you when she shares that she wrote about the *Challenger*. "How many of you picked the *Challenger*?" the speaker asks. You raise your hand. Four or five other writers raise their arms as well. A snug feeling fills you, a feeling you recognize as beyond coincidence, the momentary inclusion in an experience greater than your body, your limbs, your memories.

Later you ask a group of friends from college, "Back in first grade, at school, did you watch the *Challenger* shuttle take off then explode?" You all were born in the same year, all the same age in

January 1986. You wonder if your memory of a television show crafted your broad belief about what most children saw that day. You question these friends, all of them born and raised in the same time zone as Cape Canaveral. One is sure she watched. Another knows she didn't. Two remember nothing at all. You think about the five arms raised in a conference breakout session. You think about your friends. Maybe whatever your peripheral experiences are, they offer you authentic admittance into connecting with segments of the past. Perhaps none of these musings matter. Maybe memory is merely a fleeting fraction of reality. Yet memory forms the foundation of what you are able to tell, what people are able to tell.

*

Decades after that day in 1986, when you now live in Cape Canaveral's time zone, on an ordinary Sunday, the earth shakes. A low rumbling stirs you from the haze between fast asleep and fully awake. The tall mirror leaning against the wall vibrates. Just as you think you should run and get your daughters and stand beneath the doorframe, the movement subsides. Calm returns once more. Was that five seconds? Or maybe ten seconds? No more than fifteen seconds, you're sure. When you open your bedroom door, your youngest stands there clutching her blanket. She reports her bed bouncing and the alarm clock moving. A few minutes later, your husband says, "A 5.1 magnitude earthquake at the state border." The largest such quake in the area in over a hundred years.[7]

Your older daughter, downstairs during the key moment, arrives in your room. She heard the furniture clattering above but felt nothing on the bottom floor. A tiny earthquake. Incomparable to a space shuttle destroyed. Still, you imagine your daughter creating a memory of not having a memory that countless others may hold. Perhaps in the future, though, your daughter may also hear passing stories about the earthquake, where people were, how the shaking ground felt, what rattled in a room. Enough stories and her memory may play tricks on her mind, conjuring a recollection of standing on a trembling floor.

*

When the *Challenger* exploded, you were not in a classroom. You were not bunched with other children on a schoolroom rug. Instead, you likely leaned your head against a car window, passing vehicles gliding through winter slush. Your tummy lurched as your mother drove the great dip on Minnesota Drive and up the hill near your school. When the *Challenger* fell from the sky, it was not an ordinary day, but the day probably felt like an ordinary day for you. A day so ordinary, your vault of memories failed to sear an image into your mind. Could it be that your memory is the memory of not remembering? A peculiar-shaped, but perhaps not uncommon, container holding the accumulation of something you call the unmemories—your foggy, forgotten stories about that day.

A Moment Leads to an Essay

1.

My daughter and I share a plate of fried ripe plantains, a sweet taste that immediately reminds me of my childhood.

"Mommy, are there bananas in plantains?" she asks.

I pause. Bananas in plantains. "A plantain is a plantain," I say. "It's not a banana."

"But are there bananas in plantains?" she asks again. And I think of what she knows. The similarity in taste, the specks of black seeds. This is where the pondering begins. I ruminate about her understanding of this food that matters to her Jamaican American mama. "A plantain doesn't have any banana in it," I tell her.

2.

The memories accumulate with a ferocious speed. Plantains. Bananas. The evening years ago when my babysitter peeled a plantain, thinking it was a banana, and gave it to me. Me seated on the red stool in my childhood kitchen while my mother fried plantains. A day when I lived in Cape Town and my friend gave me a plantain picked from her friend's tree. One by one, I turn these images into fully formed scenes. As I write, I find myself wondering: "Why do I care this much about plantains?" and "When my daughter doesn't know the difference between a plantain and a banana, what does that say about me?"

3.

What is the difference between a plantain and a banana? I type those words and wait for my phone to tell me. I discover that plantains and bananas share a common ancestor that boasted much larger seeds.[1] And memories continue to pour into me. My father singing the first line from "Day O," and my sister and me yelling back the response. Family. Generations. There's something here, I think. I keep taking notes. I keep following where the memories lead. I'm not there, though. This I know. Patience, I tell myself, because patience can be what separates a glimmer of connection from a fully realized piece. Patience is sometimes just what an essayist needs.

4.

At a writing retreat, a prompt instructs me to write words directed at another human being. For reasons only my subconscious understands, I choose to write words to my sister. "I've heard it said that one day you and I will be all we have left." I write about a future day when my sister and I no longer have living parents. I write about a time when it will be just the two of us alive who experienced the memories from the early years of our lives. The free write ambles into the territory of preparation of Jamaican food and what my sister might teach me.

It's now been months since my daughter first asked me if there are bananas in plantains. It is here, though, as I sketch out this imagined scene of my sister and me, that the worlds of memory and moments, research and scenes collide in the most unexpected way. These meanderings, these questions about plantains and my daughter, this was never about what I'm teaching her. This was always about my sister, always about me. A plantain is not a banana, I discovered during my research, but they are close. My sister is not me, but we share much in common. Two black American daughters of Jamaican immigrants with different stories about the formation of our identities.

5.

The pondering began with a single question from my child. The writing found life with a long-awaited connection between two sisters and plantains and research about banana trees. In the act of understanding the connections, I began to see what mattered to this story and what might fade away. Yes to a scene of my long-ago babysitter mistaking a plantain for a banana. Yes to a memory of my mother pushing my sister and me in a grocery cart in search of plantains. No to my father singing "Day O." And no—the big surprising no—to the moment my daughter asked if bananas are in plantains. That moment began the search for the story, but it wasn't part of what the story ultimately wanted to be.

And There Will Be Imprints, and There Will Be Gifts

Knitting

My older daughter returns from my mother's house and presents me with a rectangle of knitting. A handful of rows comprised of purple, then green, followed by yellow, red, pink, blue, and teal. The stitches sag and gaps populate the whole piece. Looking at this beginner's project, I shed the years and find myself back when I was younger than this middle schooler standing before me. "Gammy said this was the first thing you knitted," my daughter tells me. A bit of string secures the final row as if to make a cape for a doll. As I touch the unintended collar, I recall the time before I knew how to overlay loops of yarn and cast off.

I knit, but I am not a knitter. As a third or fourth grader, I sat on my grandmother's bed. "Like this," she said, taking one needle, poking it through the loop of yarn on the other needle. She split the now-expanded circle with more yarn and then dipped back through the loop with the first needle. While I sat on her bed, made with hospital precision, and glanced at her miniature replica of Big Ben, she showed me how to begin. In time, my grandmother also taught me to cast on and cast off, but I never advanced much beyond a stack of homogenous rows. I knit straight lines, occasionally alternating a row of purl. Never adding stitches. Never decreasing. More than three decades since my grandmother's instructions, I now knit with even stitches. I cast on and cast off on my own. However, my knitting projects remain rectangles. Holding this tribute to my past, though, a dormant desire surfaces for a ball of yarn, the sound of needles clinking one against the other, the fibers spooling through the dip between index finger and thumb.

Questions

I own my grandmother's first knitting project. An expanse of cream, olive, and mustard. She learned to knit at the senior center the winter she left the Bronx and came to live with my family in Anchorage. She would go on to make hats and booties and even tiny sweaters sold in the gift shop to proud grandparents.

A decade ago, I used to call my grandmother while my daughter napped. In those days, my grandmother's brain had only just begun to withhold her memories. "Tell me," I'd say to my grandmother, asking her questions about her childhood or back when she was my age. I'd type her responses on my computer while she spoke of her early years in rural Jamaica. "The bullfrogs sometimes fell into the empty water tank," she once explained. "Then someone would have to swing on a plank to get them out." She mentioned the house she lived in with her mother and grandmother, a house with chunky beams she would run across from one room to the next. Sometimes she spoke about her early years in the United States, the hospital where she worked as a nurse's aide, the car named Betsy she eventually purchased.

"TC, are you writing a book?" she'd ask me. And I would look out the window, the lawn cloaking the rolling hill, her question a shadow passing across the intersection of our lives. And now I can't say how I answered. Perhaps *yes* because I wanted to mask a reality perching at the fringe of each call: *There will come a time when I will not be able to ask you these questions, there will come a time when that veil will fall.* "Grandma, were you sad when your brother and sister went to live with your father, and you stayed with your mother. Did you miss them?" She answered in keeping with her style of minimizing emotion. "What do children know about sad?"

My grandmother's first piece of knitting hung on her bedroom wall during my growing-up years. When she began the journey toward her eventual move to a nursing-home memory care unit, I asked my family if I could keep the project.

Knitting Project

After college, in the years between leaving my childhood home and starting a family of my own, I spent some time living by myself in a one-bedroom apartment near a lake. In that place, I cast on fifty stitches of multicolored yarn. A blend of purple, yellow, blue, and hints of fuchsia. I'd purchased two oversized skeins from the craft store and a pair of slim needles. In the evening, after work, when I returned to the empty apartment, I would sit on my sofa and knit until I'd accumulated six inches and then a foot of rows. Somewhere along the way, as I forged ahead with the subtle, consistent sounds of fiber looping together, of needles hurtling toward one another, I found myself unable to envision the growing creation as anything in particular. In the infancy of that project, I'd imagined a scarf as I often did. Fifty stitches, though, became too much for me to picture such a broad homemade garment twisted around my neck. My noble ambition had taken me to dizzying heights and then plopped me once more within my humanness. The six inches and then a foot, those lengths proved too large an investment in the woolen rectangle. I found myself unable to remove loops from needles, unravel what I'd already completed, and begin once more. In those fading hours of a weeknight evening, I continued, leaning back into my couch as the sun dipped and night blossomed. The rows stretched to a foot and a half. Then two feet. Finally, my eventual abandonment of the project. A point of no return had arrived where I could not imagine either undoing or completing the work. In the end, the unfinished project sat among my knitting supplies for years.

Farewell

I moved to Cape Town after I married Nyasha, the place where he'd been living for the previous eight years. Two years later, now with a baby to make us a family of three, we packed our possessions and said goodbye to that place. In the months leading up to departure, I sat on the floor in our lounge and sorted through what we'd take—most of our books, clothes, the basket our daughter slept in as an infant—and what we'd leave behind—pots and pans, our daughter's stroller, a crib mobile handed down from a friend. The open windows had left a fine film of dust, and I stared up at the burnt orange walls I had wanted to paint since the day we'd moved into that flat. But we never did. We had lived in that home like it was a transition point and not a stopping place. I touched the inexpensive couch, too hard thus rarely used. Why hadn't we just splurged on a more comfortable sofa? Somewhere in all this shuffling of goods and stuffing suitcases and selling our refrigerator and washing machine, I wondered if we were leaving too soon. Perhaps there were friendships unformed, things undone, words unsaid, lives that had never entwined.

We sold the refrigerator to someone at our church. The washing machine found a second life with Nyasha's coworker. Not long ago, almost ten years after we left Cape Town, Nyasha received an email from his old coworker. The machine had washed its final cycle of grass stains and soiled collars. It had been a good run. The time had come to bid that machine farewell.

More Knitting

Because I knit, I have walked into specialty yarn shops set along the sidewalk in charming downtowns. I have stared at the colors and fibers and imagined luscious scarves wrapped around my neck. As I've wandered toward the back of the store, I've inhaled the scent of wool wrapped in the indescribable energy of creativity.

Along with my grandmother's first knitting project, I own her copy of *The Golden Hands Complete Book of Knitting and Crochet*, published in 1973. An oversized hardback in brown with swirls of maroon. When I first turned the hefty pages to the front, I read a handwritten inscription to my grandmother dated 1988, the year after she arrived in Alaska: "This is one of my favorite knitting books and I would like you to have it. I hope you will enjoy it as much as I have." The note continued, "Thank-you for helping me." At the bottom of the page, I saw a family friend's signature. What help, I wondered, had my grandmother given to this friend? I will likely never know.

Because my grandmother taught me to knit, when I'm in the yarn shops, my imagination creates a tactile version of another life. I reach into the wicker basket of clearance yarn and allow the gentle feel on my palm and forearm to dazzle me into an extraordinary belief in what I can make. Maybe my ordinary stitches really could become much more. Only later, when I am back home with fresh yarn and new needles, do I come to terms with my own limitations—even as I begin.

Synchronicity

Some time ago, during a walk through my neighborhood, I noticed the lower portion of a stop sign lifted from the metal pole, the octagon of red secured to the top by the remaining bolt. The wind whipped tree branches. And a vision came to me of that slice of metal ripped from its bolt, soaring like a frisbee, slitting a small child's throat. I imagined octagon terror loose in my community. Later that day, I reported the faulty stop sign. "Crossroad?" the man on the line asked me. When I told him the two intersecting streets, he replied, "Of course, of course it would be my mother's neighborhood." He spoke of his mother, who lived in a house I likely passed each day. "I've been thinking for the last few days that I need to call her." His voice trailed off in the way a voice does when a person feels more words but doesn't know how to say them. "It's a reminder," I said, tempering my enthusiasm about the unexpected linking of my life with this stranger's. Too much energy might send him another way. Just before we finished the call, he said, "I'm going to call her today."

Doodle Knitting

I brought my knitting needles to my lectures during my final year of college. While my professor wrote equations at the front of the room, I added length to a scarf I never planned to wear. Knitting was less about production and more about engaging with an advanced form of doodling. Something requiring little thought to occupy me as I absorbed the engineering instruction.

Long after engineering lectures and the days of doodle knitting, I wandered into my spare bedroom. I reached up to the top shelf and pulled a plastic bin to the ground. Bags of yarn, half-finished projects, several pairs of needles. Stashed away in the closet, I preserve a shrine dedicated to unfinished projects and the ones I never began. I rummaged past the awkward scarf I created when I lived in that apartment by the lake. Buried beneath, I found a trio of crinkly skeins in green purchased years in the past. I cast on twelve loops on a medium needle, enough to yield a suitable width. And I began, prodding the other needle through each loop, wrapping the yarn around, repeating the process. Moving on to the next row. Before long, the beginnings of a scarf hatched beneath my hands. *The Golden Hands Complete Book of Knitting and Crochet* says, "The secret of knitting success lies in remembering to read through all the directions before you even consider putting needles to yarn."[1] Yet I did not know what I intended to form, the only direction being to continue.

As I knitted, my mind emptied of things that had been bothering me. Problems with friendships. Career struggles. Past regrets that seemed to plague me during seasons of stress. In place of this knotted ruminating, I focused on the way I kept tugging at the ball of yarn, pulling it into a project that would likely become nothing more than a glorified doodle, something to occupy my time. The yarn glided through my fingers and across my palm, the high grade of wool soft yet scratchy, the texture slight ridges and valleys. My needles flew just like they'd done in the past. I knitted for at least an hour. I could have carried on, but Nyasha crawled into bed. One last row and then one more before I stabbed the needles through the shrinking ball. Images of fuzzy scarves drew me toward sleep.

Weaving

Three decades after I sat in her class, my fourth grade reading teacher sent me an email. She wrote that I probably didn't remember her. I had not seen her since I left elementary school, but that instant a memory returned nonetheless. A strong and solid and firm memory unlike the wispy type, fluttering near the cliff of almost forgotten. I saw my child-self seated on the floor in my parents' bedroom reading *Where the Red Fern Grows*, trying to catch up after being home sick for three days. A robust memory that I'd thought about as recently as the other day. My long-ago teacher wrote me that she'd read some of my writing. "It had an impact on me," she said. "I have had pieces of it pop up in my mind frequently." I responded with, "Of course, I remember you," and shared the story of the novel and my sick days.

The Golden Hands Complete Book of Knitting and Crochet states, "Weaving is a method of joining two rows of stitches invisibly."[2] My teacher replied to my email with, "I had forgotten about assigning *Where the Red Fern Grows*. I only did that once." She told me that I had brightened her day.

Knitting Revisited

Long after I abandoned that too-big, incomplete, not-quite scarf I began when I lived near a lake, my older daughter and I pulled it from the storage bin of knitting supplies. For years, it had passed the time nestled near my grandmother's first knitting project and alongside the collection of unused yarn. Together we sat on my bed and unraveled hundreds of rows, releasing loops from the shape they'd occupied for more than a decade and a half. A pile of now-crimped yarn grew between us. Years after the initial creation, I could undo the work without a moment's pause. What I'd once entwined together had outlived my attachment to that initial investment. This yarn could help my daughter learn to knit. When we finished dismantling the hours and hours of time I'd once spent creating, we took the crimped yarn and wound it into a trio of balls. She packed the yarn in a bag she stores in her bedroom. Now, the yarn surfaces not on my needles, not gliding through my fingers. Instead, I have spotted the known pattern and color as hair attached to sock dolls crafted for a little sister or the unsteady knitting stitches of a beginner. I have watched my daughter sit on the couch and practice casting on.

Enough

Once I lay on a hospital bed, an oxygen tube stuck in my nose and stickers pressed to my chest to monitor my heart rate. An IV stuck into my vein. I was there for a routine procedure that required anesthesia. Vial in hand, the nurse anesthetist approached me, ready to send me to sleep. Without warning, a fuzzy memory floated into my mind about someone who never woke up from an operation. Never mind my situation differed much from a multihour invasive surgery. That morning I'd rushed from my home, hollering to Nyasha and our daughters, "I'll be back in a bit. See you all soon." I hadn't hugged my girls. I hadn't kissed Nyasha on the lips. If my life were to shortly expire, had I fed my family answers to questions they might one day ask? Had I given my girls enough that if I no longer lived, they would have a sense of what I would say, what I would do, who I was? The nurse inserted the chemicals into my veins alongside my silent prayer. No, my silent plea, "God, please let me wake up from this."

That night at dinner, I told my family the story. Even though we already knew this, I said, "When we leave each other, let's hug each other always. Let's make sure we say, 'I love you.' Let's make sure we say goodbye." I said that as if that could ever be enough.

Legacy

For my older daughter's tenth birthday, I made her a book, *Ten Things I Want to Tell You: A Mother's Words to Her Daughter on the*

Occasion of Her Tenth Birthday. I filled the book with pictures. Even more, though, I wrote stories of her life, memories of key moments, and bits of my thoughts for my girl. Now she talks of how I'm gathering stories that will become my younger daughter's tenth birthday book. *The Golden Hands Complete Book of Knitting and Crochet* states, "Details are always given in the order in which the sections are to be assembled."[3] Of course, there is no way of knowing how any of these details may interweave. Often, though, they do. And when my mind drifts into the strange realm of what could happen in life, I tell myself that my daughters will be among the ones who swell with ripe memories of years past. The ones who can stare at the monochrome of what can be winter, at the gray weather against the surface of life, and imagine the clay earth of summer, bushes the color of rose. They will be the ones who can twirl through a day and possess all it has to offer, hope drawn from the caverns of imagination. And because of all of this, perhaps I will always somehow remain.

Knitting Once More

My daughters and I stand in an aisle packed with yarn. Oversized skeins of plump, comfy strands. The classic wooly type. Crimped strands. Fibers feeling cheap and rough on the skin. Fibers cozy enough to knit a blanket destined to warm a baby. I have no plans as we look and touch the various textures. My daughters, they are the ones who arrive with dreams. My older girl wants to make a scarf for her father. My younger daughter wants to learn to crochet. So we walk up the aisle and around the next, noting colors and prices, my daughters' visions ablaze. As they pick and choose, I find myself tempted as I always am in this terrain of yarn. The ideas flicker behind every skein. I grab a purple with a gray undertone, the material smooth on my skin. In my mind, there I am seated on my couch, leaning back into the corner and casting on with no particular purpose except to knit. Perhaps I will finish what I begin. Perhaps I will not. Maybe, though, an unfinished project is not unfinished. Rather, it is merely one remnant of living.

Later, when I decide to use my new yarn, I think to flip through my grandmother's old book of knitting instruction. Knit stitches and purl stitches in various combinations yield a plethora of patterns. I want to try what I've never tried before. The book's colored images have lost their saturation over the decades, but a particular texture draws me in, the alternating squares emulating the weave of a basket. The instructions offer simple mechanics. Knit stitches and purl stitches and repeat. Several times I cast on, unravel, and begin once more. After enough attempts, a rhythm forms that I can sustain. "That's neat," my older daughter says when she sees the new pattern. "It's like that," I reply. I point to the open book.

UNDERSTANDING

A Brief Statement on Grace

My life is steeped in the concept of grace. "I believe in grace," I said several years back, during a radio interview. That day the host had probed me about two stories I mentioned in my essay collection about racial identity formation. We sat on opposite sides of the table, microphones between us. In the first story, a white man seared me with a quip about being his family's slave as I scrubbed dishes in his kitchen. The second concerned another white man, an old coworker, who made an off-handed comment about our company keeping me around for the diversity. The host had asked me, "Were the two situations the same?" My body sagged as I recalled both incidents, the adrenaline mounting in my bloodstream, my heart contracting a beat faster than normal. I held all these happenings within, though, allowing a syncopated pause to spread through the studio. The pause gave me space to formulate my response with clarity, and perhaps also invited the listeners to consider what they'd heard.

"No," I said after my verbal break. My gestures returned, helping me evoke the deeper side of these stories. The man's comment about enslavement reflected a pattern of demeaning words and responses. The second story, though, summoned my thoughts about grace. "I believe in grace," I said that day in the studio. "My coworker shouldn't have said what he said, but he'd already shown himself to be a friend. Everyone says things they wish they hadn't. I offered him grace just as I would want people to extend grace to me."

I motioned wildly as I spoke. Of course, the listeners couldn't see this, but I thought the intensity of my physical actions helped communicate my belief in forgiveness and second chances and room to make mistakes. By the time I finished with my response, my heartbeat slowed to normal.

Lately, though, I find myself wondering if I should create distance between me and the idea of grace. Where once I considered my connection to that word a compliment, now a certain degree of puzzlement gnaws at my thinking. I ask myself again and again, "What is grace? What is a gracious person?" I am in search of a definition I've discovered myself unable to name.

A note from a friend arrives in the mail. He thanks me for my kind and gracious approach when talking about race. He shares how this creates space for him as a white man to learn and is a generous gift. An email in my inbox raves, "You have so much grace and strength in your writing." A book club shares that my essay collection is full of grace. A label of *grace* stretches across my life, pulled taut by people's letters and emails, people's comments and unsolicited compliments. Firm and bold, I am uncertain how I might interact in the absence of this word pressed upon me, this word I've been known to press upon myself. With little effort, I trace the origins of my attachment to grace back to Christianity, a faith I've held since childhood. Here, grace forms the foundation for the structure of belief. Grace is seen as God's bursting clouds showering unmerited favor over humanity. Perhaps the very substance poured out from heaven, tears of rain forming, the drops soaking a dry and thirsty ground.

We equate actions with grace. Saying *please* or—more importantly—*thank you*. Writing notes, pen in hand, a few sentences of gratitude, stamp stuck in the upper right-hand corner of an envelope. Overlooking or ignoring past wrongs. Being slow to speak and slow to anger. Sometimes, though, I think grace becomes just a word we all, at times, fling around, drizzle over conversations, destined to elevate the intangible or unspoken to more. Grace. Grace-filled. Gratitude. Grateful. Gracious. Oh, my gracious. Give someone grace. Offer grace. Said with such grace. Say grace. We add these fillers to conversation and let the word serve as a substitute for an undefined concept. I know I've assumed my grace-saturated phrases emit the full fragrance of an intention I can't quite explain with concrete language. However, as more and more people—and let me be fully transparent and specify white people—have used *grace* and *gracious* to describe me and the way I approach interactions about race, how I write about racial injustice and broken race relations, the meaning of this word loses clarity. At this intersection point between this word and this topic, I think *grace* could be a euphemism for something else.

Once a white woman told me that she wanted to share my essay collection with her daughter because, "It's so important we not see color." My smile moved from genuine to forced. Another version of "color blind." A word people use in conversations about race despite the reality that medically color blind people often see some color, their world typically not a monochrome. And even if it were, they would still see black and white. My eyes settled into a slight squint. Her desire not to see color felt like a refusal to recognize my different experience. And yet, perhaps she just didn't realize how her statement marginalized me. Despite thinking this, my body resisted inviting her to consider her comment from another perspective. Sometimes the energy needed for such a reply is more than I want to exert. My—relatively— pleasant expression and lack of pushback to her remark, well, someone might mistake these attributes for signs of grace.

During a friend's birthday party, her husband mentions he listened to one of my recent interviews on a podcast. Plates of appetizers and glasses of fruity beverages, a stream of laughter and fat smiles, these items comprise our table. We sit across from one another in two long rows—distance enough that the conversation happening at the end blends into the low roar of the packed restaurant. The food is tasty. The friendships are fun. It is a day of celebration. By evening's end, my throat tickles from the raised voice I use to make myself heard even to those opposite me.

My friend's husband says, "You handled yourself well on the podcast." I think I know what his compliment means. The white podcast host asked some awkward questions about race. I appeared to answer while maintaining a positive demeanor.

While he explains the podcast to the other people on my end of the table, I tilt back in time to the day I recorded the program and sat in the metaphorical guest chair. Except I sat on my bed, my back flush against the headboard. I dialed in for the recording and remained seated in that position for over an hour of question and answer and dialogue. After the host and I bid each other goodbye, after I thanked him for having me on the show, after I hung up my phone, I slid from upright to lying on the bed, my body taking on the shape of a question mark. I lay there nursing a desire for a bowl of ice cream and mug of hot tea, a favorite movie and a pair of fuzzy socks. "I think that went fine," I wrote in a text message to a friend. "Now I'm very tired."

Back at the restaurant I explain to my friend's husband, "I can't get upset on a podcast. If I get upset, if I get angry, that only reflects poorly on me." So I attempt to choose words that the largely white listening audience—and host—won't perceive as charged or heightened. My replies offer snippets of truth while also inhabiting calm, control, composure—perhaps friendly in tone, maybe gentle enough they won't leave someone feeling bad. I spread honey butter across a hush puppy split in two, a tide of weariness returning to me as I remember the effort to navigate that hour of discussion.

"Well, you really handled it all very well," he says once more. His statement confirms the mental flips and contortions produced my intended results. But here is a fact: if that conversation/dialogue/interaction/interview exhibited signs of grace, then producing signs of grace can be exhausting.

The Old French GRACE birthed the current English usage of grace. GRACE meaning *pardon, divine grace, mercy, favor, thanks, elegance, virtue.* The thesaurus compares *grace* to *compassion, generosity, kindness, love.*[1] Pardon. Generosity. Mercy. Favor. All filmy words floating away in a cloud of abstraction. Nowhere do I find the words *gentle* or *restrained* or *lacking in anger* or *not offensive (to me)*. Often, my lauded actions do not embody any formal definition of grace. Whether some white people realize it or not, when they suggest grace with regards to race, I speculate that they often sweep *gentle, restrained, lacking in anger, not offensive (to me)* into the definition. These additions skew meaning, adding expectation beyond etymologic intent. Perhaps grace is a flaxen myth, a fairy tale reduced over time.

"Do you ever feel a weight with your name?" I ask Nyasha. I stand at our kitchen island and pack leftovers from dinner. He piles dirty dishes together and stacks them in the sink. Clean water soon fills the basin.

Nyasha's name means *grace* in Shona. Sometimes people assume his parents chose his name because of its meaning, that somehow to bestow a name meaning *grace* on their son might orient him in a particular life direction. He might then become the boy who forgave schoolboy pranks and never threw rocks. He would grow to be a man who inhabited the word *grace* when he gave a friend first choice of study carrels at the library or later, when seated around a conference table, he repeated his name time and time again for those who struggled to say it. He would be one slow to speak and quick to listen, offering a kind word more often than most. Nyasha embodies the meaning of his name. I say this, and I'm not even sure what I mean. He brings me chocolate bars, washes the dishes, stands with me in the late evening hours while together we whittle away at a pile of clean laundry. Or this, when I lose my temper or patience or both, he refuses to reciprocate by raising his voice at me. But Nyasha's parents didn't name him the Shona word for *grace* because they wanted him to grow into the word. They named him Nyasha because they liked the name. Their reasoning grants him freedom from a burden of expectation—even if he embodies qualities that might point to grace.

Nyasha doesn't dwell over my question about the weight of his name. "No," he replies, the immediacy of his response a contrast to his general pattern. A hint of mirth dangles from his answer. Laughter, I think, at what he perceives as the absurdity of such a question. Between the two of us, I am the one who harbors greater concern about the impact my words or actions may have on the peace present in any interaction. I spend time wondering if I've come across as being "nice." If grace is willing to hear beyond what another person says or offer a second chance or dig deeper for other perspectives, then I am gracious. A person who observes me—the calm voice I offer, my ability to twirl a conversation around like a prism and find light in each angle of a story, my high value on diplomacy—a stranger, an acquaintance, even a friend, could look at these specific details and label this as grace. And sometimes these qualities are acts of grace.

As I listen to Nyasha, though, I recognize myself as often searching for ways to appear less threatening when I speak about race, a sort of performance I enact during my interactions with white people. A performance couched in the perception of offering kindness. It's a flattened kindness, though, that might, in actual practice, overlook truth. Maybe Nyasha doesn't decorate his definition of grace with the excessive adornments I've contemplated.

At a writing conference, I sit on a panel titled "What Writers of Color Want White Editors to Know." I share the stage with three others. "If I read another essay by Virginia Woolf, it will be too soon," one person says. The audience laughs. I look at her, sitting next to me, and smile at what I name her fierceness, the sharpness in her tone, her refusal to structure her response with the gentle demeanor I've grown accustomed to inhabiting. I'm using a pile of notes, my answers staying close to the script I've created for myself. And hiding—I think later—behind the preformed ideas. Society is prone to view sharpness as congruent with ferocity and timidity as congruent with grace. If we shift that meaning of *grace* into concrete space, this very well might appear to be a black woman with hesitant answers and comforting words.

On more than one occasion, white friends or acquaintances have wanted to talk with me about race. We've met at coffee shops or in my living room or at the park. The friend will tell me a story about not seeing race as a child and young adult and grown woman. She tells me about her inciting incident, the flashpoint that thrust her into a differing reality than what she knew. She talks of "opened eyes" and possibly, possibly uses the word "woke." She mentions Trayvon Martin's death or the day she observed that all the children sitting at the silent table in her child's cafeteria were black. Or the time she witnessed a librarian using harsh language with a patron. Her voice begins to crack, the tepid tears swelling behind her eyelids. I might pat her shoulder and voice a handful of laments. Each time this scenario occurs, I ask myself, "How did I get here? Again?" A reversal of roles. A conversation now focused on her sadness. Me consoling another about a reality that affects my life and my body. Later, she will feel better and, perhaps, label me as gracious.

Grace is a yoke that presses me to respond with a pleasant tone. Grace is a misunderstanding of my silence. But grace is also a home where I rest my head at night. Grace is a compliment. Grace can be my goal. Grace can be flimsy and nondescript. Grace can be full and weighty. Grace is grace. And grace, often, is something else.

Be Yourself. The words on my wall fade to pale pink, old marker lines blending into the white paper. As a child, I pushed thumbtacks through my bedroom wall, securing pictures of adorable kittens coupled with messages of inspiration. All in some way, to some degree, imploring me to be myself. *Be who you are,* the posters said. Now I stick versions of those same messages on index cards and sheets of paper as if I channel a long-gone girl. *Be Yourself,* the discolored letters remind me when I pause to look. Sometimes, if I stare long enough at the words, I imagine grace resides in other spaces. Not hiding behind my timidity. Not letting my nervousness dictate how I act or what I say. As I write this, my pulse increases, and my body clenches in response to this declaration. Even as I believe this statement might hold truth, I struggle to free myself to live a different understanding of grace. I think it disturbs parts of me to discard trappings I've absorbed. Kind. Pleasant. Soft. Nice. Grace, though, must be heeding the words on my wall, acting in a way that aligns with me, and living with what happens next. Sometimes I'm gracious. Sometimes I'm not. The meaning of the word *grace* or the lack of precision in its meaning, however, need not be a yoke I carry. If grace is an abstraction, then I am a bouquet of abstractions—stems twisted, complex phrases twined—such that I cannot be reduced to a single word.

During another podcast interview, the host asked me about being a black woman. He explained that he didn't know about this because he isn't anything. By "anything" I knew he meant he's white in contrast to my black, and perhaps, to a lesser extent, he's a man in contrast to me being a woman. He continued with a few thoughts before I found a pause to counter his comment. "I'd like to push back against that idea," I said. That day I found myself answering him, and yet not him, giving a response to this question that could be a stand-in for numerous questions. In lieu of him, a stadium of people inhabited my imagination. I answered him, and I answered them. "To assume you're without a race, in fact, declares you to be normative. Then everyone else exists in relation to you." Those were not rehearsed words, and I didn't choose them for softness or intensity. I plucked them from the carousel of ideas because of the truth spinning within.

After the interview, I would question myself, wondering if my tone was off, if I should have phrased my comments in another way. For that moment, though, for that particular moment, I may have lifted myself above the ground, rising in the air. My body found a flash of emancipation from the feckless borders of a particular notion of grace.

A Small-Scale Scavenger Hunt for Sight

Please collect the following:
- *An item read more than once*
- *An idea without basis*
- *A flavor similar but not the same*
- *A garment that doesn't quite fit*
- *A piece of furniture divided*
- *A simple solution*
- *A bridge—both short and long*
- *An imagined reversal*
- *A meal near sunlight*
- *A family matter*
- *An unexpected road taken*

~~An item read more than once~~

When I am four years old, I sit at the dining room table, popsicle in hand. The flavored ice disappears as my mother reads a book about why people are different. The pages tell the story of a child's struggle to make friends at a new school. He wishes he weren't the only black student. The part of the story I love, though, concerns the boy's grandmother as she remembers her childhood. Illustrations of girls with coiled hair or braids pour from the pages. I see this part of the story dripping with the idea of a cluster of girls matching me, a pleasant puddle growing each time we arrive at that page. As my mother continues reading, my sister and I finish our sweet treats, leaving sticky fingers behind and a cold rush in our mouths. "Again, please?" my sister asks. "Another popsicle?" I add. My mother complies with both requests. Once more. Then a final time. A story read three times. Three popsicles for each little girl. And every time my mother arrives at the part about the grandmother as a child, I lean forward, taking in the illustration spread across both pages.

An idea without basis

In fifth grade, as the class waits in the hallway, my teacher tells the students we will divide into smaller groups and write raps to encourage reading. One boy leans over to announce that I should be good at this. "You're black," he says. He asserts I have a natural ability, his awkward pronouncement scrawling lines across the notebook paper of my school life. This boy knows nothing of me beyond what he sees each day in class. A quiet girl who receives good grades and whom people want in their group when smarts matter. Perhaps also when they think race matters as well. What he says serves only as a precursor of what will come my way in future years, comments about dancing and singing and tossing balls through hoops. This boy only knows the me he thinks he knows because he thinks he knows black people. Assumptions carry heft, though, and the statement rises as a barrier between me and my classmates. "No," I say, turning away, hoping no one heard what he said.

A flavor similar but not the same

In junior high school, the Patels invite my family for dinner. When they learn about their son's principal—my father—and his Indo-Caribbean ancestry, they welcome my family into their home. They serve a fragrant meal full of spice, accentuated with firm, robust flavors. Inviting aromas. Roti cooked to perfection. Food vibrant in taste. A hint of heat I cool with a spoonful of raita. The food differs from the Indian-influenced Jamaican food my mother prepares in our kitchen. Delicious yes, but not the same. After dinner my sister and I play board games with the Patels' daughter in the den and talk about school and flip through television channels. We laugh and giggle in the way and style of tween and teen girls. In between girls. Even more, our immigrant parents really raised us to be in-between. At school we buy hot lunches or pack sandwiches with peanut butter and jelly. To be us, though, is to live between cultures and customs and generations, between fading and blossoming ways of living life.

A garment that doesn't quite fit

When I am seventeen, I sit on the bottom bunk in a college dorm. Along with dozens of other students, we are here for a pre-college summer program. "Find three things you share in common," the facilitator instructs. I turn to the two other girls seated with me on the lower bunk, bare of sheets or blankets. A dorm room turned into a meeting place. We ignore the obvious complexion commonality and ask, "How old are you?" Seventeen, we discover; each of us will be eighteen in the early months of the first semester. "Do you go to church?" someone asks. As it turns out, we all grew up Baptist. "Boyfriend?" We all shake our heads. And when we announce our answer to the icebreaker, we three say in unison, "We're single, Baptist, seventeen-year-olds." Then we giggle like the girls we are.

Years in the future, the woman I remain friends with in the trio—the one who carries a bouquet of flowers in my wedding and receives a call hours after I deliver my first child—I try on this friend's blush-colored dress and discover that, as I expected, it doesn't fit. I look at her. I look once more at myself.

A piece of furniture divided

In my first post–graduate school job, I organize a book discussion after I interrogate my employer's mission statement. "Eliminating racism, empowering women," I repeat at the staff meeting. I go on to say that this branch of the YWCA actively works to empower women but doesn't do as much to eliminate racism. "How about an

'Eliminating Racism' staff book club," I suggest. So we read Marita Golden's *Don't Play in the Sun*, a memoir about a dark-skinned black woman's journey with colorism. I schedule a two-hour discussion in the conference room. The morning we meet, the people of color group to one side of the table and the white people group to the other side. Later, I debate if our moves are conscious. Perhaps when we sat down, we already knew a two-hour discussion about racism and colorism would consume the entire day. We must have guessed the exchange of words would become a skein of yarn pulled apart, too knotted up and snarled, the kind that knitters want to throw out. Maybe we could predict how our white coworker would say again and again, "I just don't understand. Why is it like this? I just don't understand." We must have chosen segregated seating because we knew how some across the table would take offense and even our executive director would appear confused.

A simple solution

Days after the book discussion, an acquaintance sits across from me in my spare office chair. For years, she has facilitated community conversations about race.

"Everyone wants to meet again," I say to her after I explain the gathering that went on all day, all day, all day. "People want to converse more. But this was hard." I want this woman to tell me what to do. I want to know what to say.

"Begin with stories," she says. She suggests I invite everyone to share a story of a time they didn't belong. "Then everyone listens to what everyone says."

A bridge both short and long

In my mid-thirties, I climb a set of stairs and stand before a podium, facing a full auditorium. Here, I pause before reading an essay about my fear as I watched my black husband drive away. After I return to my seat, a white woman approaches me with tears in her eyes, her face puffy and red. "You're just crying because you know my husband," I say to her. "No," she replies. "I'm crying because I love my husband too."

An imagined reversal

During a podcast interview, I sit on my bed. The white host tells me, "I've never had the experience of being in the minority." This experience, the hallmark of my life. Sometimes when I've heard another make a similar comment, I've attempted to imagine the feeling of a first-time encounter with being surrounded by people of another skin color. Would you look at the back of your hands and notice your wrists? Would you ponder for a time the shade of your arms compared to the color of the other arms? Would a general discomfort at being in such a situation rise within, a discomfort you might seek to repress, ignore, or deny?

"Even if you were to find yourself in that position," I offer, "your encounter would not be the same as my regular experience." And yet I think later how her acknowledgement is a beginning. Our scenarios do not run parallel. Perhaps though, there, in the flash of recognition, is where she might also consider the ways she resonates with not belonging.

A meal near sunlight

Near the windows in a waiting room, an acquaintance and I sit with our lunches. Our conversation meanders in the direction of school decisions for our children, a public magnet school for mine, a private Christian school for hers. "How did you decide?" I ask, curious as to her motivations for selecting the school. She tells me of her own childhood in the public school system and how she attended a Christian college. "I cried my first day of class," she says as she explains her professor beginning class with prayer. "I had never had that in school." She goes on to tell me that she wanted that experience for her children. A scattering of sunlight spreads through the floor-to-ceiling windows, creating rectangles of warmth but not quite reaching our seats. Silence engulfs the waiting room except for our conversation and us eating our lunches, her with her salad and me with my oversized cookie. I look at her. This being human is searching out a spot in this world where we can be ourselves.

A family matter

In late August, my father and I sit on my front porch, the sun creeping closer to our shade. The rush of an occasional car punctures the quiet. He leans back in his chair, and I sit cross-legged on the couch, waiting for him to offer me his thoughts about stories I've written about my growing-up years. "Did anything feel off? A detail I got wrong?" I ask. I'm ready to take notes. But that is not what happens. Instead, we sit in shade singed with the heat of summer, and we talk and we talk and we talk. "This is your story," he starts. Then his conversation pivots from the words I asked him to read. We talk about being a black family and an immigrant family. We talk about living in predominantly white communities. We talk about racism and our world and things that are lost. My father speaks of stories from his life. His childhood in Kingston. His late teenage years in New York City. His time living in Anchorage. He speaks of navigating a world of blackness in America as a black immigrant. He tells me things I didn't know. There is a breeze. There are birds in the leafy folds of the maple tree. There is my father. There is me.

An unexpected road taken

For my fortieth birthday party, I host a story slam. I invite my guests to share a personal story inspired by the theme of *detours*. The day of the party, the atmosphere is festive. Tissue paper streamers extend across the room and reggae music sets the mood. Bottles of wine. The savory aroma of catered food. In the refrigerator a trio of cakes from the local bakery: strawberry, almond, and carrot. Between dinner and dessert, we gather in the living room, and I share the first story. "On my way to Cape Town, I had a long layover at the Heathrow airport," I begin, shading in the background details of my true tale. I speak of needing extra pages in my passport to continue my journey. I speak of a rushed trip to the U.S. Embassy, a frantic move to fix a problem. I tell of the airline counter employee cheering me on. My gestures whirl through the air, and I know my face smiles. I conclude with a line about meeting Nyasha for the first time, "On the other side of that flight to Cape Town was the guy who would a year later ask me to marry him. The detour couldn't keep me from my destiny."

That evening others also tell stories. An impromptu vacation. A road trip in junior high school that detoured to a basketball legend's home. Someone with car problems and the kind strangers who helped her get back on the road. These are not my stories but, somehow, they become the stories of the group settled on couches and chairs and standing near the dining-room table, where I will soon make a wish and extinguish the birthday candles. The stories implant within psyches, stories of seeing one another. Perhaps, also, stories of seeing ourselves.

Breath

My love, did you hear my screams as the car hit a ditch and flipped and flipped again? The thud of metal pounding the ground. The screech of breaking glass. The way I called on Jesus until my voice grew hoarse. Those first moments, when we had no idea what happened to our daughters. The questions spilling from the haze of late afternoon. The dense crowd gathered as we emerged from the crushed car—as we *all* emerged from the crushed car. *Where are we?* I thought, pulling the girls to me, us standing on the side of the road halfway between Harare and Gweru. My toenail torn and blood dripping onto my flip-flop, a pain I became aware of only hours later. As the crowd dissipated and twilight closed in, our older daughter and I sat on suitcases, and our little one rested in her booster seat, placed right on the ground. The setting sun split into an orange and pink and lavender palette, sinking beyond the periphery of sight, replaced by a charcoal sky flush with stars. Now I can't recall turning my head upward, turning my face toward the Milky Way, saying a silent prayer that my arms held my breathing children and you walked around the battered vehicle. Thanking heavenly hosts that none of us were new flashes of starlight falling over a broken family. Now I wish I could remember the Milky Way above as we waited for Tafadzwa. The expanse of space, the pattern of stars, pinpricks of brightness barely illuminating the stoic night. The constellations of the southern sky a reminder of the great distance between here and home.

Later, I would wail. Wail for what, I couldn't place. Later, I would struggle to swallow and imagine a lump constricting my throat, my breath. I would wish to close my eyes and sleep into another century. I would find crumbs of glass on my pillowcase even though I'd already washed my hair. I'd hug the girls and—for reasons I don't understand—yell at you. Now I wish I could remember turning my head to the sky instead of staring to the bushes and vegetation, instead of watching the car lights approaching on the dark road. Because my children and you, you weren't stars. Because stars don't walk among us with flesh and heartbeats. Stars belong to another realm, the realm of deep sleep. That night, my love, we mapped a future formed from a crushed vehicle and our survival. And later, when we recrossed continents and journeyed in reverse, when we returned to our unchanged home with its nighttime view of the Big Dipper and the North Star, I would say again and again, we could have come back with one less. We could have been three. Still, there would be dreams about one of the girls, silver like a distant star, a pulse turned heavenly, glittering and distant out in space, no longer connected to the limp body that would remain. Dreams I'd startle from, the sheets drenched in my anxious sweat. I'd reach in the night for you, your breath steady and soothing, a sweet cocktail of our reality. The stars existed out there, and we all existed here. You, me, the girls, we had been passed over. Passed over. Passed over. Passed over. Life next to me. Two more across the hall, tucked in their beds. The rhythm of my own thumping heart.

My love, I can't remember turning toward the Milky Way, toward the gleam of starlight. I can't remember looking because we weren't there.

More Than Tea

1.

I used to host tea parties. A gathering in spring. Another in autumn. My invitations brought together neighbors and friends, older and younger, black and white. As the Knock Out roses began to flower or the first falling leaves drifted to the ground, I decorated a table with assorted teacups and a sugar bowl. For my menu, I offered far more than tea. Curried chicken salad sandwiches dotted with raisins. Cucumber sandwiches paired with cream cheese. Oven-fresh scones served with strawberry jam and freshly whipped cream.

The food was rich. The conversation filling. My guests looked forward to the next gathering and then the one after that. I hosted tea parties until I became the woman who *used to* host tea parties, my teacups dusty from lack of use.

2.

Once I wrote with urgency. Stories woke me from slumber, and I would crawl out of bed, grabbing my notebook or whatever else was in reach. A waterfall of words crashed against the page, my pen struggling to keep pace with the torrent of thoughts and delicate turns of phrase. I wrote, and I wrote. For years, I wrote. I wrote a book.

Then the words vanished. I slept soundly through the night, no longer shaken awake with the hushed song a fully formed sentence can bring. One night I startled from my dreamscape, not with the urgency to write, but with a stark fear that perhaps I'd written all the words out of my soul. The waterfall might not fall anymore.

Maybe I gave the words to my book, buried there and never to return. Moonlight silvered the night outside my home, but I saw nothing shimmer through the closed blinds.

3.

I think I remember my final tea party, a gathering in autumn. I baked scones and whipped peaks into sweetened cream. My guests stayed for hours, people who now remembered each other's faces, stories, names. And I thought nothing about whether that might be my last time creating such a place for more than tea.

In the final weeks of last year, my neighbor said, "Remember those tea parties you used to have?" As if I could have forgotten the plates of sandwiches or my collection of teacups or the fresh flowers someone always brought for a centerpiece. "We all loved those parties," she said, no hint of rebuke in her voice. A moment of nostalgia surfaced as we both recalled the season before I started writing my book. *The time of before,* I thought. The time of a late morning billowing into the afternoon and a table set for tea.

4.

Years after I stop hosting tea parties and months after awakening with a fear that the words have disappeared, I begin to read a book about recovering my creativity. I print sheet music to Pachelbel's *Canon in D* and take a seat at my daughters' keyboard. A seat at a piano, a position I haven't occupied in perhaps a decade or more. Another day I read the instructions to my sewing machine, remembering how to thread the needle, listening to the whirr as my foot presses the pedal. On a third day, I determine we will not dish our dinner from the counter and stove in the assembly-line pattern we assume most nights. I iron a tablecloth and set each place with a knife, fork, and spoon. The cloth napkins become flowers, and the goblets hold sparkling cider—just because. In the weeks to come, I hand letter words for a friend's birthday and try watercolors and create collages I hang from brown twine fashioned like a clothesline in an upper corner of my room. Deep in the midst of this wave of creativity joining with my life, I determine that while the season for elaborate tea parties may be gone, I will gather people over a simple meal of soup.

5.

A few weeks later, on a mild winter day, I prepare a great pot of coconut curried sweet potato soup. Everyone reaches for slices of crusty bread, the butter melting into the dense center. After we finish the meal, I offer mugs—not teacups, but hearty mugs—of rooibos tea. Conversation stretches into the late afternoon, as if to be here, to speak and to listen, enables my guests to see what is sacred in themselves and in another human being.

Early the next morning, I lace my shoes and leave behind the slight scent of yesterday's soup. As I walk through my neighborhood, I think of the flavors melded together, the creamy goodness I ladled into each bowl, the way the women asked for the recipe, and I had to explain there was no real recipe, but I could tell them what I did. With each step I take, I recall the day before. Each person's face. The leftovers I sent home with them. The hugs just before everyone departed through my front door. The aroma of ginger and the sounds of laughter stay with me. Later, back at home, I open my notebook and describe the slick texture of the soup, the color of the bubbles popping in the pot, the sound of hot tea sloshing in the bottom of a cup.

Single-Family Zoning Considered

Last summer, as the days drifted toward school returns, Nyasha and I decided to purchase our first house. Nearly a decade of living in Charlotte, and we had settled into the truth that we are here, building a life, raising our daughters, rooting ourselves into a place, turning a dot on a map into a home. Half a year later, we have scoured real estate apps and tapped hearts on features we like. We have driven through neighborhoods at midday and dusk. We have walked across swept floors and vacuumed carpets, imagining our lives unfolding in those places. Autumn spiraled into the truncated days of winter, and now life heads toward the renewal of spring. Still, we search. A shortage of housing stock and the lowest interest rates in a long time, a global pandemic and a city that ranks as one of the fastest-growing in America pour all the real estate power into the hands of the sellers.[1] Some buyers bid sight unseen, most buyers compete with multiple highest and best offers, investors throw cash offers at the limited stock only to put their marked-up purchases on the market a few months later, and everyone engages in a house-buying game I wish could be played another way. The reality, though, is we want to buy a house in a time when many other people cannot.

Every few weeks, I say to Nyasha, "Do you think we're going to find a house?" This question is incomplete. Not just a house. A house on a larger lot with mature trees. A place that reminds me in small, subtle ways of the Alaskan home where my parents raised me. I believe we will, but I wait for Nyasha's slow reply.

"Yes," he always says. "I think just a few more weeks."

I sigh a sigh that expands my abdomen. Surely, I can have patience for another few weeks.

One evening in early March, curled up on our bed, I scroll—without thought or energy—through our local NPR station's website. "Charlotte City Council Members Balk At Push To Eliminate Single-Family Zoning," a headline announces.[2] Under discussion is Charlotte's 2040 Comprehensive Plan, a proposed initiative to direct the city's growth. Despite the city's multiyear efforts to gather input from the public and later outline a direction based on that feedback, as I read the article, I'm learning about the plan for the first time.

Upzoning, missing middle density, single-family zoning. The phrases mean little to me. *Gentrification,* though, I know. A word signaling a well-worn neighborhood in close proximity to the urban core—often a victim of historic redlining—is transforming. Replaced with a glossy, high-demand area replete with brand-new half-million-dollar condos and trendy restaurants and aging single-family dwellings sold at astronomical prices, often torn down and rebuilt into houses creeping to the edges of their lots.

My elbow pressed into a pillow, I continue reading. Some say eliminating single-family zoning, the practice of allowing only one home on a lot, will let developers build duplexes and triplexes, providing more lower-cost housing options. Others argue this change will only expedite gentrification in neighborhoods flirting with flipping. And some worry about maintaining the look and feel of certain neighborhoods. A tweet from a city council member concludes the article, "Single-family zoning is a tool of segregation. If you're fighting to maintain single-family zoning, you are advocating for segregation. Stop being racist, Charlotte."[3] I'm not sure what he means.

Google informs me people across the country are considering the same topic. "Is it time to end single-family zoning?" one headline asks.[4] Another states, "Cities Start to Question an American Ideal: A House with a Yard on Every Lot."[5] The articles explain that the elimination of single-family zoning does not prevent the construction of single-family homes. Rather, the change expands the options for new housing.

"Listen to this," I say to Nyasha when he arrives upstairs with a basket of clean laundry. I grab socks and start to match patterns as I tell him about single-family zoning. "Apparently it originated in racism." How did I miss this information during my graduate studies in public policy? Or perhaps in these years since taking courses about urban renewal, highway expansion, and housing discrimination, I've forgotten. Twenty minutes into my new knowledge, though, I'm able to explain how Berkeley, California, first implemented the practice in the early 1900s.[6] "They intentionally wanted to create communities black people could not afford."

Nyasha and I, we are searching for a single-family detached home. In evenings past, when I sorted through new real estate listings, I registered the lot size, noted the tree canopy in the backyard, and wondered if there is enough room for our daughters to create another world.

Tonight, though, we finish folding the laundry and begin putting paired socks away, slipping tops on hangers, stacking sweats that we will walk in the next day. "The thing is," I say while we work, "I want a single-family home."

I belong to a black immigrant family in search of their first home. I live in a country whose collective story churns with housing discrimination that targeted people who look like me. I exist in a time when communities talk of making amends. Each of these elements tells part of a larger story, the different portions incomplete when viewed in isolation. If I dig deeper into this world that debates the merits of single-family zoning and pair my discoveries with my family's journey looking for a house, perhaps I will find what we might all be searching for.

Another evening I begin to skim the three-hundred-plus pages in the *2040 Comprehensive Plan*.[7] Nyasha and the girls move about in the background, vacuuming the remains of an art project, tidying virtual learning spaces, preparing for the start of another week of work and school. I plan to join them in their efforts, but I find myself reading rather than skimming, possibility rising from the pages. The plan states, "All Charlotte households will have access to essential amenities, goods, and services within a comfortable, tree-shaded 10-minute walk, bike, or transit trip by 2040."[8] Healthy food, parks, trails or greenways, libraries, schools, financial institutions, health care, all within ten minutes. Access to this way of living wouldn't be available to just the most resourced in our city, who can afford to live in high-demand neighborhoods close to the urban core.

"I like this plan. It's about way more than eliminating single-family zoning," I say to Nyasha. The optimist in me imagines what could happen for everyone. The cynic in me, though, whispers that it's just a plan, useless chatter constructed of photographs and words and untethered idealism.

Nothing about Charlotte's past might somehow absolve her of her own patterns of housing discrimination. She checks her share of boxes, just like most other cities, including my hometown of Anchorage. Practices of redlining, racially restrictive housing deeds, black Americans unable to access loans promoting home ownership. And single-family zoning too. Charlotte is not special in the fact that she carries this history of destroying black neighborhoods like Brooklyn and displacing residents to the West Side. Charlotte is not special in the fact that half a century later, the auspices of increased demand for urban living push those residents from their homes. Charlotte is not special in any of these ways. But for those of us who live here, this is the story we reckon with. This is the place where our city planners—with input from the community—dream about another future.

Bolstered by both curiosity and new knowledge about single-family zoning's origins in segregation, I ask my realtor, "What impact is this housing market having on inequity?" She is the definition of bubbly and upbeat. In this housing market, she reassures Nyasha and me regularly that we're going to find a home. Along the way, I appreciate her willingness to engage with my tangents. My realtor confirms my suspicions that the market we are living through now only exacerbates the already existing problems. "It's terrible, Patrice. Terrible." She goes on to mention the escalating amount of money needed and how the buyer absorbs the risk. As my realtor speaks, I hear frustration in her voice.

I think back to the fixation on the single-family zoning issue and speculate all this talk may be mere bandages pressed on gaping wounds. A wealth gap exists between white people and black people. A wealth gap created because of the history of housing discrimination and too many other shameful factors, a gap that widens with time. Yesterday's solutions included eliminating the enforcement of racial covenants and ending practices of redlining, both of which did little to reverse damage.[9] Today's solutions include ending single-family zoning. Tomorrow's solutions will be something else.

My realtor and I spend almost an hour talking on the phone that morning. I sit at my desk, staring out my window at the suburban sidewalks and my neighbor's tree, many of the dead autumn leaves still clinging to its branches.

Single-family zoning leads to segregation because, statistically, black families are less likely to have that escalating amount of money enabling them to purchase such a home. Reduced access to home ownership means reduced access to building generational wealth. In the end, casting aside single-family zoning may do little to remedy the injuries inflicted by this city's and country's forefathers. If the average black person fundamentally has less money than the average white person, how can anything really change?

"I want a single-family home," I say—just as I had said to Nyasha.

"Of course you do," my realtor replies. "It's the American Dream." In Charlotte, single-family zoning swallows 84 percent of the land.[10]

"Is it wrong to want a single-family home?" I ask Nyasha one morning. "Wrong for me to want a lot that reminds me of my childhood?" Maybe looking for a single-family home equates with acquiescence to an unjust system seemingly beyond my control. I, like so many others, have been conditioned to want this thing one city council member called an American tradition.[11] A tradition born of another American tradition—racism. Nyasha converses as he rummages through the closet for sweats and a T-shirt. We leave the question without an answer, heavy and fogging my thoughts throughout the day.

My immigrant parents arrived in this country with little. When I was six years old, they purchased the house where I grew up, a red house with a black trim, four bedrooms with an unfinished basement, at the end of a gravel road. Our first summer in that house, my father repainted our new home gray edged with a smoky blue. "Can I help?" I asked. He grabbed a can of paint, and I followed him to the low laundry room window in the backyard. "Like this." My father's brush drew a smooth, even line. In the shadows cast by towering pine trees, amid the chalky odor of paint and steely scent of green, growing things, I added a crooked trim to a place no one would ever see. Pockets of blue pooled as I painted the house my parents owned—a house that belonged to them and belonged to me.

Later, as I prepare dinner, Nyasha returns to the morning's question. "I don't know what it is," he says, "but I want to own land that is ours, something for us to have. Something we could leave for the girls." Somehow the margins and pauses speak an answer extending far beyond any American Dream. In Zimbabwe, the white settlers once pointed a gun at Nyasha's great-grandfather and forced him to surrender his best cows and relinquish his land.

"Of course you do," I reply, "when so much has already been lost and so much has already been taken." Likely, my own wants are motivated by far more than an Alaskan childhood on a one-acre lot. Oddly, now we are looking to buy a house built on stolen land. In Charlotte this land was first occupied by the Catawba people.[12] If we fall back across history, this land was never something we could own.

A Saturday, and the heady warmth of early spring bleeds into the lingering chill of winter. Entwined with this hint of new life, a hesitant anticipation pulses through me as Nyasha, the girls, and I visit yet another neighborhood. The picture on the real estate app revealed a symmetrical blue home with a redone interior.

As we drive through the neighborhood on our way to the house in question, I notice a worn and well-lived appearance. Solid structures in need of updates. This remodel, though, comes priced far beyond the expected value of the neighborhood. We circle the tight cul-de-sac and arrive just as a black family finishes their tour and exits. "Look," I say to Nyasha, mentioning what we are seeing for the first time, another black family in this search for home ownership.

And later, after we walk through the house and the girls marvel at the two staircases, after we peek in the garage clutching the strong scent of fresh paint, after I stand in the backyard, the near-spring sun warm on my forearms, after I consider where the furniture might go, after we finally leave, I think back to that family. Maybe they wanted to make an offer. If that might be true, I don't want to be their competition in this quest to access another layer of the American Dream. Perhaps they looked at us and thought the same thing.

Weeks pass, and we notice the house closes for $20,000 above the asking price.

Nyasha mentions a podcast he listened to about housing discrimination: "Over the last forty years, black people have accumulated an average of $200,000 less wealth compared to their white counterparts."[13]

What he says sends me back in time to last autumn and a cool morning when I sat outside speaking on the phone with a friend. "Come to our neighborhood," she said when I told her about our search for a home. I thought about her walkable life, the local restaurants just blocks away, the grocery store up the street, the library across from there, the location near uptown Charlotte. According to all the trends, a desirable area. Also a place, though, with clusters of homes where a little searching might reveal racial covenants attached to archaic deeds. Unenforceable, overlooked words like, "This lot shall be owned and occupied by people of the Caucasian race only."

Rather quickly I responded to my friend's fun suggestion with, "We can't afford to live there." That day, I rushed past my comment, my words embarrassing me. Even if I might have wanted to consider the possibility of our children walking to each other's homes, meeting each other on bicycles destined for a nearby ice cream store, Nyasha and I would be stretching ourselves far beyond our budget to afford my friend's housing life. My mouth soured, and shame came for me. Who wants to verbalize that in this way one may differ from a friend, never mind that our races already illuminated that reality. Studies indicate that even when controlling for level of education and income, a white person is more likely to own a house than a black person.[14] The neighborhoods where they tend to purchase are not the same.[15]

Of course, there are stories behind each person's placement within broader statistics. A multitude of variables. Skin color alone cannot explain all the reasons one person can afford a neighborhood and another can't. Still, that night when Nyasha mentions the $200,000, months after I spoke with my friend, I can't help but—rightly or wrongly—apply the data to my life. An extra $200,000, and maybe we could have considered a house near my friend.

It takes my family and me almost an hour to drive the entire outer ring road on a bright Sunday in early spring. "485 is generally shaped like a circle. Not perfect, though," I explain to my older daughter, who studies circumference and radius in her math class. "But we can find the circumference and estimate a radius for Charlotte."

Early on, we pass a large patch of Callery pear trees, flush with fragile white petals, a tree historically planted in suburban communities across America. The species invades now as it migrates from beyond the confines of planned streets.[16] Soon countless recently established subdivisions come into view. These neighborhoods help house a city that has more than doubled in population in the past fifteen years.[17]

And there are hotels and hospitals, chain restaurants and car dealerships, office buildings and open space and, in some places, an abundance of trees. Occasionally we whiz by land stripped of brush and foliage, bulldozed and bulldozed again, the earth turned over, wooden skeletons standing, waiting for construction workers to add floors, walls, a roof. Someone once told me she loathes neighborhoods like these. The appearance of sameness built one after the other. Perhaps she didn't recognize that these neighborhoods, in recent years, have become sanctuaries for many people of color looking for an affordable entry point into the housing market. New construction on the fringe provides options.[18]

What I can't know now, as we circle the ring road, is that a few weeks in the future, on a mild spring morning, butterflies flitting through my view, my shoulders will rise at the hope of a home. Nyasha will touch the newly replaced kitchen countertops, and the girls will claim bedrooms. Outside, standing on a pebble path in the shadow of poplar trees, I will see what might come to pass in this place. Our family gathered with friends, roasting marshmallows around a firepit. The girls on their graduation days, the parties lasting long into the night. Amid those swirly ideas about the future, Nyasha and I will offer $17,000 above the asking price, modeling that number on the premium given to a house sold a mere month ago in that same neighborhood—determining we will not escalate the price further. We'll add a letter detailing our family's love for both the home and the botanical garden–inspired backyard. Most of all, we'll dream. But our offerings will not be enough, and the sellers will go with another buyer.

Now though, weeks before that disappointment, we continue our drive around our city, and I think about how, several years ago, Charlotte celebrated its 250th birthday. At the time, a radio commentary mentioned that if history repeats itself, 250 years in the future hardly anything standing today will remain.[19] I try to picture all these buildings gone, the three malls I spotted no longer there, old and new neighborhoods vanishing across time, a not-yet-known dwelling for my family transformed to nothing but dust.

I'm tired of impotent solutions, I think as I stare at the changing combination of landscape and cityscape. What I want is this way of living brought to ashes, floating away in the wind, releasing the opportunity to start once more. Instead of plans incessantly working to remedy the enduring legacy of all these past wrongs or half-heartedly attempting to repair what never really worked before or pretending that merely ending previous discrimination practices will offset the effect of generations of state-sanctioned injustice, I want us all to somehow start from nothing. Then we can imagine the beginning of a world different from what we grasp now. This type of thinking populates dreamscapes, though, grounded in what is impossible, what is not real.

Toward the end of this drive, which arose from curiosity about circles, the far-off uptown skyline climbs above the treetops. I mention the view so Nyasha can glance to the right. In the back my older daughter stares out the window, but my younger daughter has drifted off to sleep. The structures silver a patch of space, human-engineered peaks prominent against the cloud-filled horizon. Within a moment, as our journey around 485 continues, the perspective shifts. The treetops grow once more. Or the skyline shrinks in height. Or none of this happens, but I am not in the place I just was. For a drop of time that removes me from the world as it is, I think that perhaps a day will come when what is here now will no longer exist.

The Blooming of Mournful Things

Colors

A cluster of dandelions pokes through the scraggly grass hugging the side of my home. Not quite the variety of my childhood. Tall. Thin. Almost fragile in appearance. Absent the thick stems I remember staining my skin. Perhaps these interlopers aren't even dandelions. My younger daughter reaches for what she calls flowers, clumps them together in her fist, and hands me a child's bouquet. "I love you too," I say in response.

More than three decades ago, I spent time plucking dandelions from the width and breadth of my front yard. Overnight their trademark yellow appeared, the weeds pushing through the earth, dotting the carpet of green. These tiny sunbursts, though, were not akin to daffodils adorned in beauty, radiating the day's warmth as I sometimes imagined. That summer, I leaned over the lawn, my back hunched as I yanked at the would-be weeds, piling them in a pail. My parents paid me a penny for each dandelion pulled, and my aunt, distant in the mysterious land of New York, doubled my wage. I never tugged in malice, but my motions removed each eyesore from the ground that had given it life. The broken stems left dandelion milk on my fingers and palms, sticky and darkening as dust and dirt coated the remains. Sometimes, not often, but sometimes, I snapped a dandelion with the yellow flower grayed to a fuzzy puff. I brought the plant close to my mouth, formed my lips into an O, and offered a soft breath that loosened the seeds. The breeze carried my wish out into the distance and the quiet wilderness of trees.

With a paring knife and my thumb pressed against the top, I strip a thin membrane from a stalk of rhubarb. I've eaten rhubarb my whole life. In breads and crisps and strawberry-rhubarb pies. Stringing rhubarb, though, is a first. After I finish, I chop the stalks into nickel-size pieces. Then I add strawberries, husked and split in two. Finally, I pour sugar over the top, the crystals dissolving within moments. Only later, after I remove the dessert from the oven, do I recall the thickener I forgot to add to the filling. A river of deep pink floods the gap vacated by the first scoop of the warm cobbler. This texture disappoints, replicating nothing I know.

In the patch of world where I was born, fresh rhubarb grew along the sides of people's homes. Those were places of oversized elephant ears for leaves and scarlet stalks masked beneath the green and vibrant possibility of what might delight. A family friend used her rhubarb stash to bake perfect pies, where the insides bubbled through the crust and sometimes dripped over the edge. "A sign of a good pie," she would say. I spoon my too-thin cobbler into my mouth. Just a forgotten ingredient. Remedied next time. Still, as the tang and sweet touch my taste buds, I think only of pies I once ate.

"I want to burn these," I say to Nyasha, holding a thick stack of old meeting minutes and spreadsheets and bulleted lists. This is where I once lost too many nights of sleep. A time on the board of an organization. An internal crisis I tried to help fix. Yellow flames will ignite the paper, consuming evidence of a season now past. "I want to burn these," I repeat. Already my imagination is reducing what I hold to nothing. Later, Nyasha drags the charcoal grill from the shed and lights the coals. I place the papers in the metal belly.

As it turns out, printer paper resists flames. The edges brown and the fire dies, nothing catching. Nyasha pours lighter fluid, and I begin afresh. Now the flames rise in their own spiraled dance. Smoke clouds the air, the odor of burnt paper sinking into my hair and clothes, eclipsing the scent of the trees and grass, forcing me beyond the path of the haze. The breeze is fickle, though, and wisps follow me. When I rustle the pages with a grill fork, a gust rises, stinging my eyes. The movement brings the fire's renewal, and the growing pile of ash continues to belch smoke.

In the end, when the fire fades, I find a word or phrase here. The bottom of a spreadsheet there. The flames have retreated from evidence turned not quite to gray.

The cardinal appears in spring. More likely, though, in spring I notice his scarlet body loitering on a fence slat. Or sometimes as the faucet fills a pot in the sink, my eyes lift to the wooded area behind our home. A flash of red disappears into the budded leaves. One day, I take a pencil and sketch my crimson friend. With my watercolors, I bring his shape to life, a blend of oranges and reds and brown. A bit of black near his beak. Shades of green grow the leaves surrounding where his feet hook around a branch. When I investigate the bird's etymology, I find his name originates from the word *carde* meaning *hinge* or *that upon which it all depends*. All that is to come depends on what has come before.

Objects

A dinner bell used to hide out in different places in the kitchen when I was growing up. The window ledge just above the sink. The brown cabinet hanging over the orange countertops. The lazy Susan where the cough medicine stayed. I think my mother bought the bell envisioning herself wiping her hands on her apron while the scent of curry chicken and thyme leaked from the pots at the stove. I think my mother thought she would take the crystal bell from its resting place. With a flick of her wrist, the tiny ball would strike the base of the bell. A quick, repetitive ding would travel with the food's full aroma to all corners of our house, announcing the time for dinner. I think that's what my mother envisioned. A bell would chime. A family would eat.

As it was, the little bell spent most of its time hidden away in the cabinet as my mother rushed through dinner preparations and my sister or I banged plates and silverware into a set table. Replacing a tinkling ring, I would scream, "Dinner," to my sister or she would scream the same to me. We would find our seats at the table, absent my father because he had to work late. Every now and then, though, maybe at a Sunday lunch, my mother would tell me to ring the bell. I'd reach for the smooth handle, shake my hand, and let the shimmering sound summon our family into the most pleasant of memories.

Saved over weeks or perhaps months, a pile of newspapers grew in the swatch of space between my father's nightstand and my parents' bedroom window. My father would snap open paper sacks from the grocery store and place the brown bags on their sides. Each time our family finished reading the *Anchorage Daily News* or the *Anchorage Times* or even the *Jamaica Gleaner*—the slim newspaper that arrived not in plastic sleeves tossed on our driveway, but in our PO box, the paper an already out-of-date indulgence that connected my immigrant parents to their home—each time we finished reading, my father slid the newspaper into a bag. One on top of the other until the bags bulged with past news of Anchorage and Alaska and America, of Kingston and Jamaica and the world. And when my father had accumulated a stack of bags stuffed with old newspapers, we carried them to the garage, the crumples and creasing flooding our hallway and staircases, the aroma of ink, newsprint, and unbleached paper sticking to our clothes. We loaded the newspapers in the back of my father's pick-up truck, the words and stories on their way to the recycling center to be reborn in an alternate life.

Now I am grown, far from childhood and far from my place of origin. Far from the days when the *Anchorage Times* closed their doors after printing their final afternoon edition. Far from the forgotten moment when my parents ceased their international subscription to the *Jamaica Gleaner*—enough years having passed that they no longer needed outdated news of a first home. The *Anchorage Daily News*, though, remained, morphing for a season into the *Alaska Dispatch News* and returning to the *Anchorage Daily News* once more. We lived our lives. We grew older. I moved far away.

In adulthood, I call my father and apologize for sifting money from what he once collected. He used to save what most people never saw in ordinary circulation: silver dollars, fifty-cent pieces, two-dollar bills. The coins made their home in a Ziploc bag near the washed-out margarine tub—the storage place for ordinary quarters, dimes, nickels, and pennies. Everything resided in his bureau, the scent of money seeping into the room each time someone pulled open the top drawer. And when no one was watching, I pilfered coins. I began with the quarters and dimes. In the absence of those, I slid my hand into the plastic bag and reached for a silver dollar, cold and slick and weighty in my palm. For lunch money because I didn't want to pack a sandwich. For a comic book that found a final resting place in the recycling bin. For a temporary future of satisfaction that I would fast forget. I spent my father's collectable coins on nothing that would last.

"It's okay, PT," my father tells me. He says this to me, and still I cannot rid myself of the images of those coins, the heft of them in my warm hand.

I tell a near stranger about how, as the days of summer vacation faded, my parents used to give my older sister and me a budget for new school clothes. Just before my sophomore year, my sister traded in a shopping trip to the mall for yards of fabric from Joann's. *I want to make my clothes,* she said as she pinned translucent brown paper on bold-patterned material.

The story continues with the night before the first day of class. My sister knocked on my door. A pile of periwinkle spilled from her arms. She held up pants with an unfinished hemline and pins stuck in the seams. *Can I borrow some of your clothes?* she asked in a voice frayed and heavy from days of sewing. Across the hallway, through her open door, I could see pins, pinking shears, and half-finished pants and skirts strewn across the floor. I turned back to her face and shook my head. She looked down at the fabric and crossed the short distance between our rooms. I saw the flash of light blue fabric just before the door closed behind her.

I tell the near stranger that I don't think my sister even remembers the incident, but sometimes I see myself crossing the hallway, knocking on the door, and offering her my new blue leggings and striped sweater. "I wish you could forgive yourself," the near stranger says. In telling her this story, perhaps I do.

Voices

In the familiar photograph, my mother leans back into the corner of a floral couch, my baby body resting in her lap and my head tucked in the crook of her arm. Her face is tilted down toward mine, and perhaps she croons a made-up lullaby formed from part of my name. "Tricie, Tricie," she sings, lulling me to sleep.

My mother told me she liked the name Patricia, the way it sounds with the three syllables offered to the air. "But I wanted something a little different," she explained as she relayed to me the story of my name. She dropped the final syllable along with the "sh" sound, a wisp of breath close to the slight noise one makes to hush a small child. Not Patricia. Patrice.

I think my mother knew that while she wanted to hold her baby close and rock her into a full night of sleep, she also wanted my arms to one day reach wide and my legs to travel far. I like to imagine she dropped the "sh" sound because she knew there would be too many places where I would need to make my presence known. She could not have known then that a day would come, decades later, when a therapist would say to me, "You need to find your voice. You need to use it and say what needs to be said." In the photograph, my infant self snuggled into the warmth of my mother. That night, my shrill sobs surely called her to my crib.

There were dolls in my childhood. A doll with brunette hair and a plaid dress. A blond doll with high-heeled shoes that I lost. A magic doll whose lipstick appeared when I smeared a sponge dipped in hot water across her pale face. And one doll, a doll my parents had found after scouring one store and then another and another, searching for a match for their daughter. A brown baby with dark hair that I would weave into braids.

There were also dolls I made in school. A doll I painted off-white, attaching hair fashioned from yellow yarn. Or the doll I constructed in art class, taking a preformed body made of cream-colored cloth and using scraps of fabric for her skirt and top. No one offered and never once did I think to ask if I could make a doll that looked like me.

In high school, I began listening to pop music, tuning the dial on the clock radio perched at the edge of my nightstand. Nicki French's cover of "Total Eclipse of the Heart," Sophie B. Hawkins's "As I Lay Me Down to Sleep," All-4-One's "I Swear"—which gave me fodder for my adolescent dreams about the boy with the floppy brown hair that always knew the answers, just like me. And there was Michael Jackson's "You Are Not Alone" and Meat Loaf's "I Would Do Anything for Love." My friends and I would sit around at lunch discussing how despite Meat Loaf's seven-minute ballad, no one could name the "that" that Meat Loaf wouldn't do. We said this with a laugh because at fifteen, of course, we were smarter than the musicians. And at sixteen, when I was able to drive myself around, selecting radio stations with the tip of my index finger, I would often belt out Lisa Loeb's "Stay," waiting for that one perfect line about naivety—just because I liked to say the word *naïve*, having no idea how naïve I might be.

Decades later, sometimes that music will find me over a loud-speaker. As I fill my cart with groceries or peruse the racks at the thrift shop. When the familiar notes from "Stay" catch me unaware, without even realizing it, I begin to hum along. My body tips into a slight sway, and I add my off-key voice to the entire song.

Before I arrived in the city where I make my home, I heard a message in a dream, *There, there is a friend waiting for you, one who needs you just as you need her.* In that new place, I began looking into the faces of the people wandering into my life. I searched for that friend that needed me too. I believed in the manifestation of that dream as if it were bestowed with vertebrae and wings and fresh chances, alive and real. Often though I discovered, yet again, that another friend perhaps was not the dream friend. A day came when I began to doubt that dream had once arrived in the purple hours of night.

In the patch of years since I determined I had, long ago, loaded more meaning on that sleepscape than it could bear, I have turned my gaze back across the decade. I stare in the direction of what I once lived. All I can see there in the middle of my life is myself. "Perhaps you are your own soul friend," someone suggests. Perhaps the friend waiting for me, the one who needed me as much as I needed her, perhaps, all along, this woman has been me. I bring my hands together as if one is reaching for the other.

Locations

In the final burst of late afternoon, the back roads charm me with expansive fields and an occasional brick home. "I hope the wedding finishes before dark," I say to Nyasha. He agrees and maybe he envisions what I imagine I might see: these fields and forests masked beneath dusk with us alone on a deserted road.

Later, when there is pop music and a sky of stars, when there are slices of cake and lanterns aglow, I try to laugh when I tell our white friends about my concern about my family driving down a dark road. "Do you want us to follow you to the highway?" they ask when Nyasha and I decide it's time to go. I shake my head, but then I stop because I want to say "Yes, please," instead of defaulting to "Thank you, but no."

Nyasha and I left a church once. We said our goodbyes to a community of people after several years of sharing crockpot meals, babysitting their children, and praying for one another. We left because Sunday afternoons, as we drove home, steady tears rushed down my cheeks, chubby droplets leaking abandoned beliefs. This cruel realization cut into my skin, drawing blood. "I think we have to leave," Nyasha said, and I agreed. Who I was becoming, who *we* were becoming, was not who they were. To stay was an impossible thing.

Many years later I had a dream about those people and that place. A radiance saturated the scene as if we stood in the golden hour prior to sunset. The copper glow buoyed the undertones of faces I saw and people I greeted. My former pastor's wife reached for my hand and hugged me. Near the front of the sanctuary, a seat waited for me.

When I awoke from that dream, a strange energy ran through my body, filling my veins, warming my arms, and strengthening my legs and feet. I knew I'd shed whatever hold that place once had on me, and I was floating. Perhaps now I could visit that place again. I would marvel at how the children had grown. I would smile at all the people I'd never before seen.

A writing residency in rural Minnesota, and the first hints of morning sun draw me from my room. In those fresh hours of day that I share with a handful of deer and a couple of storks pecking at worms, I follow the curvature of a calm lake. Dew covers the wild grass, and the tangy aroma of pine needles tickles my nose. A strange familiarity crushes me, the relics of my Alaska past dripping into this present moment. The cool of morning. The particular variety of trees. The scent of the water nearby and a packed trail and the enduring certitude of the outdoors.

Another morning, my walk takes me down a nearly deserted road. At the corner of my vision, a known object appears, transporting me firmly to another era, another place. A newspaper box at the foot of a stranger's yard. A blue background. Eight yellow stars. I read the words *Anchorage Times,* trace the image of the Big Dipper, and behold a sight I haven't seen in twenty years. When I turn toward the house, set back from the road, I stare in a way that might make the structure reveal its secrets and connections to my home. I touch those stars just as I once touched the ridges of a spruce trunk, rose hips, mounds of snow. As I walk away from the plot of land, my arms open to clutch the feeling of wilderness emanating around me. My mind softly sifts through a life now out of date, the life of long ago.

We are brave at this house. We are loving at this house. We have fun at this house. My older daughter chalked those words on the path leading to our front porch, ribbons of color backed by dulling concrete. The driveway boasts four stick figures and a house with three windows. We are brave. We are loving. We have fun. At this house. In this family. My body trembles, and I bring the heel of my hand to my eye.

Once I lived with my parents and my sister and my grandmother in a gray house trimmed in blue at the dead end of a dirt road. The perimeter of the yard mingled with the woods. A swing set. A strawberry patch. A bent-over birch that became a climbing tree. In that house, we sat in our living room and created teams for Pictionary. In that house we spent Saturday night in the family den, watching *Star Trek: The Next Generation.* In that house we let the needle drop on old records, scratching out songs from my parents' youth.

And when my parents' marriage ended, they split the furniture and the photo albums. They divided the dishes and the money. They dissolved their "we" and my "we" as well. Once I lived in a house at the end of a road. We were brave at that house. We were loving at that house. We had fun at that house.

Shadows

A forgotten black cemetery shares a border with a pristine playground. On the other side of the lovingly laid wood chips and plenty of park benches, a tumble of overgrown foliage hides graves belonging to the long deceased. A pair of birds cruise the apparent emptiness before soaring into a mammoth tree. Squirrels break the quiet as their feet crinkle dried leaves. I am the only living human here. And I spend my morning walking among the departed, the shrubbery spines scratching my bare calves. I wind my way through the tall grass and pause at gravestones battered by weather and time. A dear mother lost. A child dead at age three. Another on the day of his birth. A man killed in the Spanish American War. A woman named Mamie.

A wrought-iron fence divides graveyard from playground, shaggy from manicured, near-silence from sound, death from life. Swings and slides constructed of plastic and primary colors. And further afield, a neighborhood in flux. Fresh homes, new paint, white joggers, a blond woman pushing a stroller. I retrieve two bouquets from my car, purchased an hour before at the grocery store, dividing them into smaller bunches and single stems. Back in the cemetery, I weave once more through the tall grass, laying carnations and daisies in front of tombstones, placing fresh flowers over the remains of black bodies buried beneath the ground.

My father died twenty years ago today, Nyasha's text message reads in the midmorning hours. He watched a body given to the ground, a soul departed. And somewhere, a hemisphere away, I knew nothing. I slammed my locker after first period economics, scratched out precalculus problems on notebook paper, read glossy brochures from colleges on the other side of my country, across the Atlantic from his. His father was dying, and I saw the gray of my high school and plotted a future of picturesque lawns, sprawling trees, college textbooks held snug against my hip. Ten thousand miles split the us that existed then as him and as me. His father whispered words into his ear. Shallow, warm breath against his skin. A root, a memory to touch, turn over, feel again and again. My husband's body heaved with a now-adult sigh, and the dust clung to his good clothes. We couldn't know then the way time zones would collapse, the way beating hearts would crush distance. Twenty years gone, and now in the late-night hours I whisper in his ear, cup my fingers in a circle and speak, with the sound of the living, what I think echoes from the grave. *You make me proud*, I say. I wish for a voice I never heard, a deep tone I can create only in dreams. A voice he knew twenty years ago.

To the right of my childhood home, where the grass melted into a thick wood, our tree's steady wooden arms embraced two sisters and their imaginary games. I remember low branches covered with lichen and soft moss, just a foot or two above the dark soil. The dip between branch and trunk served as a sort of woodland lap, a seat to welcome even the most unlikely tree climber. From early morning, we slid our hands across peeling birch bark while our feet peeked from beneath a cap of bright green leaves. By day's end, sticky brown sap stained sleeves, palms, and pant legs.

One year my parents spent a chunk of their savings replacing a decaying septic system. From their accounts, a chainsaw came to cut down our tree and the wood around it. Then a bulldozer arrived to turn the earth and bury a new tank. Gone was the heady spice of pine needles, birch leaves, and a breathing wood. Replaced with the dull smell of packed dirt.

Later, after it was all done, my mother bought a bucket of wild-flower seeds for us to sprinkle across the bald ground. We never did. Not that spring or any spring after. Now whenever I see fields of wildflowers edging the highway or curling around an old barn, I stare at the purples, reds, and oranges stretching wide. I pretend

I remember the feel of thin petals brushing against my ankles, the scent of color brought to life.

In spring we let the raised bed in our backyard sit fallow. The soil remains forlorn and untilled, the bags of purchased dirt absent, the seeds untouched on the garage shelf. By summertime, when I peer out the window at the drying grass, I have nothing of the planted variety leavening the season with anticipation. No sign of heirloom tomatoes changing colors on vines. No taste of the sweet harvest paired with balsamic vinaigrette. Instead, weeds grow in what has been our garden. Untamed grass and spindly plants.

One morning, I clip roses from one of the bushes beneath the kitchen window. Winding its way between the leaves and pink petals, a green vine twists toward the sky. A dollop of cherry tomatoes dangle from the plant. Tomatoes among rose bushes and far from the raised bed where vegetables should grow. I reach for this remnant of seed spread the previous year when a bird pecked at our garden. In my cupped palm, I harvest what might nourish, something wild to eat.

CHANGING

What Is Common, What Is Rare

The early August weekend that hate groups marched through Charlottesville, Virginia, my eclipse fever vanished. Just over a week before the first coast-to-coast solar eclipse on the North American continent in almost a century, my Twitter feed and BBC app exploded with too many images.[1] White supremacists gathered in the streets of a city less than three hundred miles from my home in Charlotte—another namesake of the same English queen. Instead of considering the upcoming movement of the moon and rather than searching out the perfect patch of earth within the band of totality, I stared at pictures of crowds. Torches and raised fists condemned the removal of a Confederate general's statue. A young man thrust a flame before him, his face growling with chants and slogans and the shape of hate. Each time I saw that particular photograph, my shoulders tightened, wanting to prevent a shiver from coursing across my body.

A few months before, when I'd learned about the upcoming solar eclipse in late August, giant surges of energy and curiosity had drawn me into an ongoing search for information about the day. I pulled up digital maps and studied the gray line beginning in Oregon and sweeping across the land, exiting the continent near Charleston, South Carolina. Charlotte sat outside the band of totality, in the common world of partial eclipses, just beyond the sixty-mile-wide strip of land that could bear witness to a total eclipse. As a child, I'd witnessed a partial eclipse, but everything I read told me this couldn't compare to experiencing a total eclipse. So each time I looked at the digital maps, I focused on this path of totality. I traced the band with my finger on the computer screen.

I made notes of all the cities and towns within the border, a ripple of daytime darkness moving across the country in two-minute bursts. To view this, we couldn't stay in Charlotte.

The summer prior, I'd left Charlotte and spent time in the mountains of North Carolina, breathing in the fragrant and fresh air as glorious and pure as people say. And during my time in those mountains, I wrote. For days, I wrote. One night, toward the end of my stay, I stood at a podium beneath bright lights and read a short essay about being a black woman married to a black man. I looked up from my page and pretended to make occasional eye contact with the audience. In reality, though, all I could see were the images my words created. "Please, my love, keep your hands on the wheel, your registration close. Keep your speed under the limit and go straight home."[2] With the slightest shake in my voice, I read those words about watching Nyasha drive away.

The following year, during that summer of hate rallies and solar eclipse fever, I received an email from a friend titled, "An Issue of Concern." She'd heard a white person read a piece of their own work. A white writer from Virginia—perhaps not Charlottesville, but Virginia nonetheless—who'd been in the audience the night I'd shared my essay.

"As far as I could tell, it was simply your words appropriated, twisted, undermined," my friend wrote of this other person's piece. She went on to say, "I cannot believe you would have condoned such appropriation, and I most certainly doubt you are even aware of it." She included a link to where the piece had found a publication home. I knew my friend wouldn't lie, but how could what she said be true?

*

The obvious difference between Charlottesville and Charlotte is six letters. S V I L L E. Those six letters declare one a city of possession and the other a city of veneration. Charlotte's city versus using Queen Charlotte's name to memorialize a place. That summer

I wondered if substantial differences existed between these two places. The Sunday morning after the Charlottesville headlines, another friend sent me an email. "I'm praying for Charlotte," she wrote. "It was bound to happen," I told Nyasha during the car ride to church when I mentioned the error.

When we arrived, my girls headed to the children's classrooms followed by Nyasha, who was helping in the nursery. I sat in the sanctuary wedged in a corner near a window flush with streaming daylight. I checked my email before the service started and found a follow-up note from my friend with an apology for her mistake. *But Charlottesville could easily be Charlotte*, I thought, and I knew this was true. I knew some people sharing this city with me and my family spoke of heritage and not hate. They talked of preserving memorials. They asked me, as a black woman, to understand how preserving this legacy of slavery was not the same as hate.

*

The last time I'd seen a solar eclipse—not total, just partial—I was eight years old. My third-grade teacher had shuffled my class out the side entrance of my elementary school in Anchorage and handed us each a pair of special glasses. It was March. The frigid temperatures of not-quite spring leached the heat from our bodies. "Look now," my teacher said. The circle of the moon moved in front of the sun, leaving the sun in the shape of a crescent.

Decades later, my smile grew each time I told people about the band of totality bringing approximately two minutes of twilight in the midst of an ordinary day. I wanted to stand within that band. I wanted to be in the dark while it was day. I wanted to see the moon settle in front of the sun, our perfect moon, the right size and distance from our spinning planet to give the illusion that this mass of rock is the same size as our sun. I longed to see this moment of alignment between heavenly bodies when twilight descended and the signs of time flipped in on itself.

What Is Common, What Is Rare   125

As I considered the upcoming eclipse, my mind pondered that essay I'd written about watching Nyasha drive away. I'd taken parts of my experience, pieced together images and aromas of the mountains, of an art gallery, of Nyasha's hand holding mine. I'd formed something drawn from deep places in myself. I'd offered those words to a room of white listeners. A white writer in that audience heard my words, used part of my story, and formed something derivative that they'd named their own.

I wrote the editor who published this white writer's piece. I included a link to my own essay, exposing the parallels. I explained how the other author knew me and—more importantly—my work. I talked about the perpetuation of injustice of allowing a white person to take my story about race and use it to benefit their writing. The editor told me that I'd made this a black/white issue. *That is unfortunate*, the editor added, sandwiched among the rest of the lengthy response.

*

I often think the silver nights of August lack true rest. The temperatures oscillate between stuffy and a little too cool. My dreams rouse me from sleep at an hour long before the first hints of light. Before dawn wakens, I live in the in-between spaces of my world, the time when my part of the earth spins toward the gold of the sun, and the reflected sunlight illuminating the moon begins to fade. Before dawn wakens, I think of flowers closed in on themselves, curled in a state of rest. Before dawn wakens, whatever I carried with me into sleep the night before, whatever thoughts weighed me down, seem lifted, as if forgotten, not made new with a new day, but instead ignored, pushed aside—a momentary sensation that challenges don't exist and that goosebumps are not truly a sign of the cold.

On an early August night much like that, after I stared too long at men raising fists and holding flaming torches in the darkness and chanting words I was thankful I couldn't hear, I shook Nyasha's shoulder.

"Should we move?" I asked. I wasn't sure what I wanted in response. An assurance that Charlotte wasn't Charlottesville, that fear was far away, that whatever we read about could not creep into the life we carried out in this city we referred to as home.

"Maybe," he said. He turned on his side, his breath slowing back to sleep. In the splitting silence of all that happens between twilight and the waking dawn, I kept my palm on his shoulder and lay awake waiting for the creak of morning.

*

In the days after the Charlottesville events and leading up to the late-August eclipse, I noticed people began to reorganize their lives around a moment in time. A mounting connection with strangers built as I overheard conversations about viewing spots and day trips into the path of totality. In Charlotte, we existed beyond the edge of what was possible, but near enough we could go and take part. How odd, it seemed, that this unusual sight would settle across the width of the country, and we wouldn't be able to keep from turning our gaze. A moment of time when the earth, the moon, and the sun formed a perfect path of alignment. A moment of syzygy. *Syzygy*, derived from the Greek *suzugos* meaning "yoked, paired." And in a way, all of us who plotted perfect viewing spots were yoked or paired with the events that would unfold above us in the sky. Through the special lenses, we'd lift our heads upward. When the anomaly left, the heavenly bodies and starry hosts would return to predictability, limbs of outer space no longer tangled together. Instinctively, we'd return to shifting our gaze from the sun and protecting our eyes from the severity of the light. We'd return to our lives, the sun continuing to hold the power to blind us with its rays. In the absence of the moon's covering and the special lenses, we would once again turn away.

Somewhere in Virginia, a white writer took something from me. A personal story that I'd shaped into an artifact. The lived experience I'd chosen to share. After several email exchanges, the editor never conceded any form of wrongdoing. The closest thing to an apology came when the editor informed me that the author of the derived piece was sorry I was upset. Is a created work like a living being formed from a skeleton, fit together with muscles, sinew, and flesh, presented as a breathing entity with its own reason for existence? Perhaps so. Maybe what this person did in deriving work from my essay was attempt to take the beating heart of this living work and try to reconstruct it with foreign bits of flesh.

Unfortunate, the editor said about my attempts to address the situation. With those words, I retreated from the conversation and waited for the moment to pass. I believed another person couldn't eclipse the heart of my creation.

A few days before the solar eclipse, my family and I left behind the scalding, sticky summer days in Charlotte and spent a morning in the mountains tugging tart apples from the arms of an orchard. When we'd finished, we drove a short distance to a little café that made fresh sandwiches and thin-crust pizzas. On our way, we passed a road named for the same Confederate general whose statue—or the planned removal of whose statue—served as a catalyst for the riots and marches. I looked at the sign and then turned my head away.

*

The day of the solar eclipse, my family and I drove to a small town just north of Columbia, South Carolina. We parked in a field across from the town park and joined a handful of other people in the shade, wandering to the open expanse for occasional views of the moon's movement. For over an hour, we went through the acts of putting on our glasses and looking up and looking away until there was but a sliver of orange in the sky. Then black. The temperature dropped, and the summer day turned to evening against my face. We stood in the longest shadow I'd ever known, the shadow of the moon across the earth. When I looked again through the glasses, the orange sliver of sun just there had disappeared. For two minutes, darkness akin to twilight enveloped us. I removed my glasses and told my daughters to do the same.

Totality. The moon surrounded by the sun's corona. For a moment, just a moment, a ring of pale purple light. We stood in that shadow amazed by a sight that, of course, would not remain.

And on that day, perhaps not in that moment though, I thought about a white writer in Virginia who'd lifted something from my life and derived words from the essay I'd already used my voice to tell. *Please take those words down. Please remove this more than inspired work,* I'd written to the editor. The work remained. At some point that summer, I realized I was weary—just plain weary—of pointing out the problem and hoping someone would make a change. In truth, I chose to slink away.

I knew I would give readings in the future at independent bookstores or on a college campus, at writing workshops, at places where I would be unable to know who sat in the audience. I'd flip through my unpublished work, and I'd wonder who might be out there taking notes about what I would say. What is it that we are aligned for? Why do human orbits cross and what shadow might fall without humility or concern, refusing to let my world return to order and predictability?

That August, I believed in the days, weeks, months, and years to come, the monuments and memorials paying homage to a past riddled with the practice of slavery would disappear from public life. Sometimes one at a time, sometimes in large groups. In the totality of this moment in history, I believed we would see fallen statues and ripped-down signs. We would hear voices that spoke of choosing not to look away. On a future apple-picking excursion, I wouldn't pass a road sign named for a general who fought to ensure certain human beings lived out their days trapped in slavery.

Despite the general solar eclipse excitement and anticipation, it's a misconception to believe that this phenomenon is an unusual event. In fact, a total solar eclipse occurs about every eighteen months somewhere on our planet. However, it had been almost a hundred years since the last *coast-to-coast* eclipse tumbled across the width of the United States. That afternoon we stood in the midst of what is common and what is rare.

Days before, hate groups had marched publicly through city streets. When that moment in history would continue on its orbit, moving beyond a time of syzygy, when the vigils ceased, candles snuffed and songs of resistance quieted to their typical pitch, our world would still be left with white writers who use a black woman's story—and editors who defend those choices. We'd denounce the marches and torches and chants. When that moment passed—as it surely would—we'd continue to live with the ghosts of our country's peculiar legacy. A reality that hate groups marching through streets cannot eclipse.

Out in that open field, gathered with strangers, the opposite sliver of orange appeared, a stark reminder of the temporary nature of totality. All around arms raised and returned those glasses to our eyes, the moon continued its orbit, and the earth did the same. The moment of syzygy slipped away, replaced by the shimmer of late afternoon.

We took one last look at the growing crescent of sun, now in reverse of what we saw prior to totality. We took our blanket, our glasses, our family, and piled back into the car, joining the crowd of eclipse viewers winding their way up the highway, headed toward Charlotte. Vehicles disappeared in the distance, backing the highway up for miles. Inside the cars, people surely swapped eclipse stories and had eclipse glasses and worn picnic blankets and knew that the cars ahead and behind and on either side all had the same. By the time my family pulled into our driveway several hours later, the moon had moved out of the path of the sun. We returned to our home beneath an ordinary light.

Our Words at a Moment in Time

After I returned my first essay collection's approved edits to my publisher, a momentary burst of triumph washed over me. Then worry began to creep into my celebratory mood—worry I tried to banish with the purchase of a book, a necklace, and a donut too. When I'd first turned in my manuscript, I had believed I'd written the best essay collection I could possibly write. Several months later, while reviewing the suggested edits, I spotted adjectives I needed to cut and several paragraphs I found excessive. I rewrote a metaphor and changed the word choice in more than a handful of places.

Now there will be no more revisions. There will be no more changes. The words I returned are nearly the same words I will see, later this year, printed on the pages of my book. In the interim, however, I will continue to write and read and study the craft of writing. As a result, the writer I will be when I open my book will not be the same writer I am today. The writer I become in the future will have a greater ability to see the flaws in my work. And this fact scares me.

The rush of triumph—and the celebratory donut—doesn't negate the worry that one day I may find my work wanting.

*

Once I had the opportunity to participate in a writing residency at the Collegeville Institute, a week of quiet, peace, and solitude on a college campus in rural Minnesota. I woke early each morning and took a walk beside a lake, sharing the new day with several deer and a couple of storks. The sun rose above the water, streaks of pink and orange staining the horizon and radiating with what I considered to be writing inspiration.

One afternoon I took a break from working on my essay collection and visited a nearby pottery studio. The manager invited me on a tour. As he spoke about the history of the studio, I stared at a row of rounded vessels almost—but not quite—identical in shape and style, the damp clay dark gray. Full, leafy branches twisted around the curve of each vessel—except for the last one. Here I saw what the other pots would become, the branches soon removed, revealing a delicate pattern imprinted into the clay.

"We have a three-hundred-year supply of clay," the manager said. He talked of generations in the future when other artists would use the same source of clay the studio uses now. He mentioned how the presence of the clay reminds everyone that the studio is not one artist. The studio arises from the collected work of many.

I was taken with this idea of enough clay to last three hundred years. Long after we are all gone, a potter none of us would ever know would throw pots made of the same material. Immediately I thought of a verse fragment from my Christian faith. "We are surrounded by such a great cloud of witnesses." A great cloud of participants in a long creative tradition.

*

A three-hundred-year supply of clay. I return to this idea now in the aftermath of approving my edits. I try to conceive of the vast number of objects artists will create over the lifetime of a three-hundred-year supply. But I also remember those branches with full leaves pressed into the bodies of a row of vessels similar in shape and form. I recall the one vessel with the visible imprint.

Is it possible to feel both small and significant in a single moment? Because I do. The medium I throw on the blank page is not part of a lengthy—but finite—supply of clay. Instead, a supply of words without end. A reality that scoops my work up in the ongoing legacy of writers before me and writers not yet born.

Perhaps what is true is that when we look back on work we wrote four months ago or four years ago or, eventually, four decades ago, our contributions may seem flawed and inadequate if considered in isolation. Perhaps some degree of all we create will, at some point, fail to reflect the writer we will become—even with our greatest triumphs. That one vessel with the leafy imprint offered a fleeting beauty that pales in significance to all the work that will ultimately originate from not just that potter but—more importantly—also from that supply of clay. But the thought of that vessel alongside hundreds of years of created pottery made me gasp.

Maybe we find the freedom to let go of worry about how we will perceive our words in the future through the act of seeing our creation as one artifact that is part of a greater whole. A contribution to both the words written before and the words that will come after. It is not perfection that defines the worth of my contribution. Rather, it is the willingness to offer to this ongoing creative tradition the best work I can as the writer I am at a particular moment in time.

Two Field Guides

Field Guide to the Unraveling of Your Interracial Friendships

To start with, you need to accept that you are here because you and your white friend decided to talk about race. This choice produced problematic consequences. Otherwise this might merely be called "Field Guide to the Unraveling of Your Friendships." But you're here. The topic of race has surfaced. You engaged in discussions beyond the harmless acknowledgement of your different shades of skin.

You and your white friend tiptoed before leaping into talk about the presence of systemic racial injustice. Together you considered how society's marred and sad history around race casts a troubling shadow over the present. You exchanged opinions about the shooting of unarmed black men, disparities in education, the potential for the first black president.

No matter which white friend, when she said, "Give me examples of how race had an impact on your childhood," you sliced open old hurts and shared stories of being a little black girl in a predominantly white environment.

Then you nodded when your friend said, "I've always wanted to be friends with black people."

Since you liked the person you sat across the table from, since you discovered you wanted the friendship to develop, you chose to ignore it when she said, "I felt just like that once when I was around a group of really wealthy people," in response to how you felt when all the little girls were doing hair at the slumber party, and you didn't get to take part. You decided to overlook the time she told you, "I don't see color," because you believed—and why shouldn't you have assumed the best?—that she didn't mean she didn't see you and your brown skin. What you hoped she meant was that she formed friendships based on character alone. The statement, though, made you feel like the wide sweep of the dominant culture wanted to brush away pieces of your identity. But you kept these things to yourself. You knew your words might make her uncomfortable and make this friendship falter.

What you couldn't know is that overlooking something just means shoving your hurt inside, shoving it so far down you don't even know it exists. This, of course, will have its consequences too.

Which is why, one day, a conflict will develop between you and your friend. Not about race. About something petty like the fact that she doesn't answer your emails or the way you whine when you are sick. The issues will appear trivial to the outside world, but they will be dense rain clouds over your friendship. As you try to sort out these frustrations, you will both discover new things to be annoyed about until it just seems easier not to be friends.

Of course, the real problem is your conversations about race, the way she made comments that made you shrivel, the way you felt it better to ignore statements than discuss them. This is what leads to irrational levels of irritation about the unimportant. However, you won't yet recognize how the mind shifts conflict from the uncomfortable issues to the ones that seem easier to address.

And when your friend says, "I just don't understand" (which, of course, she will say since you're in conflict about a substitute conflict), you will sit and stew and rant and rage.

Still, somewhere deep within you, in an almost hidden place, you will wonder what you can do to fix this. Is there a way you both can once again sit across from each other over steaming drinks and hear the air saturated with the sound of your laughter?

Field Guide to Reconciling in Your Interracial Friendships
One day when you are glancing at a burst of wildflowers along the highway or tugging towels from the hot cave of the dryer, your drifting mind will puzzle through the disintegration of your

friendship. In that unexpected—perhaps even supernatural—moment, bright signs will point to the truth that this wasn't just any friendship that disintegrated. This was the disintegration of an interracial friendship. Only then will you recall the way your friend told you how her experience was similar to yours. Only then will you remember the words your friend said that made you feel small. Only then will the memory of remarks that you overlooked in your effort to be gracious gush from your mind in the form of warm tears.

Now is when you start to understand all the conversations you had, all the easy thoughts you shared about injustice—in all this you missed the fact that with white friends who want to talk about race, you have a greater chance of sinking. You think everyone is fine and comfortable. Then you realize this friend who is your good, good friend can say things that hurt you, can make comments about race that burn. You see your mistakes. Maybe you should have just circled around the topic, never really stepping into that conversation, the same strategy you use with most of your white friends. You could have talked about other topics like weekend plans or favorite books and thus remained in safer realms.

But the divine spark of recognition has found you, and now you know race is at the core of the problems with your friend. Now consider your friendship. Think about her qualities that are wonderful. Think about if you want to keep the friend. Observe if you have some sort of nagging feeling that there might be something to preserve. As will sometimes happen, you may realize that you're okay if this friendship glides away. If so, just embrace this truth as an unexpected gift.

If, however, you believe in preservation, here is where you can make several choices. You can continue to ignore the statements your friend made about race that bothered you and slap a Band-Aid over the relationship. Call your friend or write an email and apologize for your nutty behavior and anger over inconsequential issues. Then tell yourself that you need to check your responses and conjure up a bunch of gracious feelings that overflow from your soul in calm, quiet, and even conversation.

(It is important to note that if you choose this path, the path without rocks and bumps and large potholes, in the future you will again read the "Field Guide to the Unraveling of Your Interracial Friendships." You will then wonder how you got here once more. That's okay. Repetition of experience may usher in greater understanding.)

Alternatively, you may decide this friendship matters and honesty should leave little room for Band-Aids and quick fixes. If that's the case, now you need to wait for time to do the thing that time does best: pass. And have patience. Have lots and lots of patience because repair work can be slow. On both sides of the friendship, whatever hurt exists needs to soften. Even if you long for everything to resolve, value the silence that might stretch from weeks to months to beyond a year. Think how this gives you time to mull over the friendship and the casual way you both spoke about race. Be thankful for the space to sort through why you felt unable to tell your friend when her words hurt. Perhaps she will be doing the same thing. In these silent times, the friendships meant to last will separate from the chaff.

Remember patience. The waiting might give you hope that this story will find a way to continue. But you should know that there is never a guarantee. If relationships are like wine, some get better with age and some become no better than vinegar. Keep praying yours becomes the one you want to drink.

Then just maybe one day, on a random Tuesday afternoon, in the near or distant future, one of you will decide to pick up the phone, sit down at the computer, or knock on the other person's door. The air will smell fragrant. Time will reach an unexplainable point of being "right." Contact will happen again. And you will both discover yourselves to be changed people.

Together you will begin talking, and this time you will embrace an uncomfortable authenticity, speaking the words you once hid. A conversation here. Another conversation later. Even later a longer conversation, maybe stretching into the dark night. Together you will see how your friendship—your interracial friendship—began to disintegrate. You and the other person will accept that as much as you don't want to be people who hurt their friends, you both wear the cloak of humanity. When it comes to discussing race, the risk of wounding each other becomes high.

You will remember, though, why once upon a time you saw her cream skin, she saw your brown skin, and you both wanted to stay. As you talk over weeks or maybe months or even beyond a year, you will understand that racial reconciliation can't be reduced to a list of what to say and what not to say. It might be the intentional journey to discover the experience of another person, another culture, another part of the human race. Woven in with all the mess, you and your friend will get to touch this profound beauty. If that happens, run your fingers across the fibers of this life, touching each unique thread, knowing your friend touches a different version of the same.

My Pandemic Days: March–July 2020

"Did I do that?" Steve Urkel asks, his voice slightly nasal, his expression almost bashful. Moments earlier he walked into an office. As the door slammed behind him, the window glass cracked and fell to the ground. Then he tripped, becoming tangled in the macramé plant holder hanging from the ceiling. In his attempts to free himself, he pushed a statue through the window of a high rise. Another version of the same antics my family and I have been watching for the last four months. Just as in evenings past, a deluge of laughter fills our living room.

Four months. The time since *Family Matters* re-entered my life. No longer packaged as part of the two-hour TGIF line-up from my childhood. Thanks to a global pandemic, the show has returned as my family's default evening viewing. Like the Winslows, many nights Nyasha, our daughters, and I gather in our living room. While the number of cases, hospitalizations, and deaths rises, we cycle through several episodes centered around this multigenerational family and their annoying—but lovable—neighbor.

I remember our last true evening of moving through life with a sort of carefree abandon I wouldn't have been able to name then and can only begin to fathom now. On a Friday evening in mid-March, I took the girls to a park shortly before sunset. My daughters chased each other around the playground, launched themselves from moving swings, and released a string of shrieks while speeding down slides. While they played, I walked around the park and stepped over shallow roots and looped dirt paths winding between trees. Around me, the timetable of my community had begun to soften as the spreading virus shifted people toward home. Toilet paper was in short supply, and I considered the notion overdramatized. As I circled the park's perimeter, I spoke on the phone with an old friend.

"We're going to binge-watch a nineties sitcom," I told her, explaining our plans for what I thought then were the coming weeks. The sun disappeared beneath the tree line and beacons of golden lights glowed in homes beyond the park. I finished the call and continued to walk beneath the moon, silver against the wine of the deepening sky. When the girls and I left that evening, we never thought to say goodbye to the park.

Now it is mid-July. One morning my elderly neighbor and I speak as I near the end of my daily walk. He sits on his front porch, a crossword puzzle in his lap. I stand well over six feet away, at the end of his driveway. Summer sweat soaks my T-shirt, but people talk of what will happen with school in the autumn. Virtual platforms? Masks? School buses? I share the varied opinions, and he says, "Keep them home. They can learn later." By *them*, he doesn't mean just my children. He means all the children. Hearing him speak is hearing my own ruminations voiced. Whether I've been aware or not, I recognize my silent expectations. Whatever happens with this pandemic, and its devastation across the globe, by August, the time of school returns, I thought we—the people in positions of authority? the community? all of us occupying this world?—would have this sorted. These days, though, I speak not of weeks or a few months. Now I speak of next summer or next Christmas.

"This has shaken us out of our complacency," my neighbor tells me. I don't ask him to explain further. Instead, I point to the flower garden extending across the width of his front yard. Purple. Pink. Yellow. Red. Broad petals. Petals the size of dimes. Stems rising skyward. Plants unfolding just above the ground. The scene of these abundant blooms flourishing within ordinary patterns and seasons gives me pause, beyond my response in summers past. "Those are beautiful," I say. My neighbor nods. I depart, the distance increasing as I continue on my way.

In those early days back in March, I stared out my kitchen window at the white laundry pegged to the drying rack. Inside, dish suds and tepid water soaked my skin. Outside, a breeze ruffled Nyasha's T-shirt and tugged my older daughter's tank top into the air. The window above the sink framed a picture of white. The clean clothes. The fence enclosing the backyard. The blossoms soon to be leaves in a cluster of trees. A view of spring saturated in a single color. Our dryer was broken. Those days, though, those days were not days when we called repair companies and allowed others to enter our home. My new routine became placing the wire rack on the lawn and letting the sunlight suck the dampness from the clothes. Later, I'd carry inside a full laundry basket smelling faintly like the outdoors. As the girls and I folded, we'd listen to YouTube videos of the *Family Matters* theme song. While we sorted socks and slipped spring tops onto wooden hangers and stacked the girls' leggings in a pile to take to their room, we'd belt out the lyrics to "As Days Go By." Other days, they'd imitate Steve, twisting their own voices to sound like him, pretending to trip over the laundry basket or knock over a tray table. "Did I do that?" they'd say, and we'd grin at the parody, a welcome respite.

In an episode of *Family Matters*, Steve straps a jet pack to his back and launches himself upward, breaks through the ceiling, and crashes through the Winslow family's home. High in the clouds, his body surges through the air, the Chicago skyline swelling in the backdrop. Outside the small-screen world, we laugh from the couch, from the chair, from our positions as observers. We laugh and laugh. We laugh even as we knew this would happen. A storyline where Carl and Eddie fix the roof. Steve with a jet pack. The emphatic expectation gallops toward completion in the final scene. For long ago, we learned to collect clues and we learned to see. Steve glides across the sky, and we suspend disbelief. Absent are the voices that might whisper, "Is that even possible?" "What about the reduced levels of oxygen?" "How will he land?" We arrived in our living room with a desire to smile and wash our worries away in the comical hum of hypnotic jubilation. The show is predictable. Now, I think, predictability is what we crave.

Another day, Nyasha and the girls call me as a storm approaches from the south. My oldest appears in my makeshift office. "Mommy, the rain's coming. Do you want to sit on the front porch?" My family knows my evolving rhythms and routines. I didn't used to seek out a view of a descending storm. In the past, I found enough contentment in listening to the cacophony of drops against the rooftop and ground below.

"These months," I tell Nyasha, "I stare." Stare at what I'm not sure. I settle into the patio loveseat and wait. Distant claps of thunder. A crack of lightning. The sky darkens to slate. The humid temperatures cool. A storm approaches, and I sit here waiting for what I know will shortly unfold. A gale sweeps through, shaking the trees, sending my neighbor's garbage can into the driveway. Branches buckle and the hard wind claws at leaves. Then the exodus of water descends from heaven, and the strength of the downpour bruises the bald patches in my front yard. For a time, I sit on my patio furniture covered, sheltered, the rain mist wetting my clothes, leaving a film on my skin. Finally, the wind blows the raindrops sideways toward my viewing sanctuary. I grab the blanket I'd spread across my lap, open the screen door, and return to safety. After another ten minutes, the wind subsides, the tree branches upright once more. The slate sky dissipates to bright sun and the clearest of blues. The overturned garbage bin serves as the sole remnant.

These days rainstorms call to me because I'm struck by the consistent power of the natural world. The unending days press on, add together, multiply upon themselves, and I gather stories of the earth's pandemic transformation. Views of the Himalayan Mountains that people haven't seen in three decades.[1] Pictures of the transparent canals in Venice.[2] Lions spotted napping on a road in Kruger National Park, absent vehicles scouring the land for sightings of mighty beasts.[3] I collect these stories of the shifting planet. Clear water, clean air, content animals. Changes revealed by the slowed pace of human life.

"We on the earth suffer, and the earth heals," I say when I speak to friends, just as mystified as the previous time I shared this thought. I make the comment as if to speak those words might reveal a transformative insight guiding me toward some larger meaning for this sorrow reaching across the globe. Nothing surfaces. So, in another conversation, with another friend, I'll try again. Other days, I wonder if the earth has failed all of us. This mass of stone and dirt whirling in space, kept in orbit by the pull of a star, perhaps we held expectations for what this planet might be for all its inhabitants. In Yosemite National Park, a coyote roams its own habitat without the greedy intrusion of humans.[4] Maybe I held expectations for this earth, expectations I didn't even know. Even more, perhaps the earth held its own expectations of us. And we are the ones who betrayed our home.

Sometimes, though, I think of these days like satin stitched together, seam after seam after seam. The smoothness as I trace my fingers across the expanse of one earth rotation blending into another, laced together with the reality of the disease existing now. The ever-present tick of a clock reminds us that we splice together fragments and moments to create our acts of living. A dreary morning. Two girls seated at a table with pencil and paper. Art projects in a symphony of color. Dinner in front of an old sitcom. Each moment sewn together into what has become this version of life.

I find there are moments I want to preserve even as I imagine and perhaps hope that our lives will loop back to some aspect of the way we were. When the girls launch into another sibling cycle of "Stop that!" "Stop that!" "Leave me alone!" I find myself without my typical elevated response. A calm tone appears, asking, "What's happening, girls? Do you need help?" Or I just ignore their words to each other. There exists time to accept that these arguments will soon disappear, without my assistance. They always do. I used to think I'd lost my ability to manifest patience, that my low voice and casual response had trickled out of my body. In these months, I've discovered that streak of impatience drifting far, far away. There are family nights with popcorn and *Family Matters*. There are bicycle rides and early morning strolls. There are marathon sessions of Rummikub. There are nights of stargazing complete with sightings of Jupiter. These days, these days might also be a pile of pure gold.

I had a dream where I donned a mask, and beneath the cotton layer, I couldn't breathe. Everyone around me sported the same apparel. As I think of it now, we all must have been gasping for air to fill our lungs. In my dream, I struggled to inhale, exhale, and repeat. In actual life, I wrote those words on a piece of watercolor paper and taped them to the wall near the family desk. A reminder to anyone who pulled up a chair there. Inhale. Exhale. Repeat. Just breathe. For breath is something one might take for granted and forget the possibility of infusing with intentionality. I wear a mask now when out in public places. As I wear my mask and recall that dream, I discover my own challenges with breathing.

Two months into this pandemic, which exacts a disproportionate impact on black and brown communities and black and brown lives, a white police officer pressed his knee on George Floyd's neck for over eight minutes. Eight minutes where a human being cried for his mother. Pleaded for his life. Struggled to inhale, exhale, and repeat. In the aftermath, protesters cast aside social distancing and stay-at-home orders. They donned masks and surged into city streets across the country and around the world. Crowds carried signs, walking in unison, shoulder to shoulder. Each time I saw an image of one of these marches for justice, my eyes took me right to the masks snuffing out facial expressions. These people who marched, though, could inhale, exhale, and repeat. They didn't have a knee compressing their air passage, denying the human need to breathe.

During that time, I coiled inward, not answering phone calls or returning text messages. I woke in the morning with numb arms, a manifestation of my stress. I found myself struggling to leave my bed. And when people asked how I was, I said, "I'm not doing well. I am not doing well." When others asked me what I thought, I recognized I had nothing new to say. What I might think, I had written before. My black husband driving away. Keith Lamont Scott's death. The Charleston Church Massacre. I disappeared behind the words I'd already said and wondered if my retreat had become just another mask.

By chance, somewhere in those weeks following George Floyd's murder, we watched a rare episode of *Family Matters* steeped in gravity. A pair of cops pulls over Eddie, targeting him for being black in a white neighborhood. That night sighs riddled my reaction. To watch such a storyline from twenty-five years ago is to know sorrow. As the familiar situation unfolded, several looks and a handful of hushed words passed between Nyasha and me: "Still the same," "What changes?" This episode happened then, and this episode happens now. Beyond the boundaries of our home and the perimeter of our neighborhood, protest exploded in a time of a pandemic because our world refuses to allow all access to air. In a dream, I wore a mask, and I couldn't breathe.

At the end of June, an editor I've worked with in the past called me to ask about my recent writing ruminations. For over a month, I'd followed the reality of the largest racially motivated protests since Dr. King's assassination in 1968. While others had shared articles on Facebook or participated in community discussions or chanted outside police stations, I'd spent much of the previous month huddled in varying degrees of grief and despair. The editor's call arrived just as I found myself more and more able to return from my retreat. Last year the magazine had published an essay I wrote about Keith Lamont Scott's death and the destruction of Charlotte's old Brooklyn neighborhood. Some days when I thought about that essay alongside George Floyd's murder or Ahmaud Arbery's or Breonna Taylor's or an endless list of lives curtailed, sometimes I wanted to weep.

"Where are your thoughts going?" the editor asked.

I spun out ideas consuming my thoughts. The ways in which entities and individuals preserve history. Midlife as well. "And the pandemic, of course," I added. "I think too much about the pandemic."

"Yes," he said. "But what is there to say now?" Beyond preserving stories for the future, he went on to add. Truth existed in his statement. On the other side of this, whether weeks or months, I would be able to look backward in an ordered fashion and search for meaning rising from the chaos. Now, I was simply doing the living. Only later did I recognize myself dissenting from his view. Even in this moment, even in these months of uncertainty, even in the midst of living something that seems without end, I had words to write. These musings lacked a requirement of the complete passage of a moment in history. Life continued to manifest in me and around me, illness knotted with injustice. And somehow in this parched and thirsty season, the unexpected also pushed through the earth.

As I type these words in July, I hear my daughters speaking to friends on Facetime. A pair of sisters they used to see nearly every day at school. Their friendship has transformed to one of video calls and occasional handwritten letters in the mail. I hear my oldest scream, "You did? Have you seen Steve Urkel yet?" And I know in another house here in our city, another family is disappearing into the feel-good comedy of a nineties sitcom. "Did I do that?" my youngest says in near perfect imitation, the show's catchphrase connecting the sibling sets. Giggles come from the girls' room and through the screen as well. A few minutes later, the four girls begin to sing the words to the *Family Matters* theme song. I recall how months ago, when watching the Winslows felt like a novelty, my daughters and I sang the song together over and over again. Now we're far enough in the seasons that the show has dropped the opening theme. I haven't heard "As Days Go By" in quite some time. Even as we continue to watch, aspects of *Family Matters* are already fading into pandemic memory.

In the early weeks of the pandemic, in the first month or month and a half, I crafted an essay about my family and our new habit of eating dinner while we watched *Family Matters*. I wrote about escapism and the desire to find refuge from the mounting statistics. I wrote about creating some sort of imaginary bubble of safety— all the while knowing the world is not safe and never has been. I wrote those words and then did nothing with that essay. Within a week, the changing face of life eclipsed the essay's relevance. The words lost their punch, and the ideas fell into the realm of out-of-date. When I reread the essay now, the fragment of time I captured seems suspended within the archaic past of a world morphing each and every day. This fact both pains me and emboldens me. I can only imagine that one day the warp and weave of what I preserve here will also drift into the tired timbre of yesteryear. I write this, though, to say that I could not have imagined these days continuing to rise on the horizon. I have not hugged a friend in months. I find myself with little expectation of when I will.

My older daughter comes into my bedroom, where I'm preparing the virtual class I'll teach that weekend. "Mommy, there's a deer stuck in our fence." I run downstairs to the sliding glass door and stand with Nyasha and our younger daughter. My older girl watches from the kitchen window. In the backyard, a deer struggles between two slats. Her rear end protrudes into the free space beyond the fence. Her front legs and head and upper body remain trapped within the confines of our yard. She shakes her legs and jumps in the air, trying to yank the balance of herself through the narrow space. Each pull forward must tense her body, and I imagine her brain releasing an abundance of cortisol and adrenaline. I see her eyes, and I see fear.

"Go backwards. Go backwards," I whisper through the window even though she cannot hear me. I want to believe my words can and will travel on sacred sound waves to reach her ears. She continues, though, with the impossible task of wedging her stuck body into what she'll come to realize is just a cage.

"This is sad," I say to Nyasha. My older daughter agrees. The weak rays of early morning bathe the deer's brown coat in a glossy shine. Cream spots dapple her side. There must be other deer out there waiting for her return. "Go backwards," I whisper again.

This time she does.

First shifting her legs in reverse, then scrambling a bit to maneuver her torso and rib cage through as well. Then she stands on the other side of the fence, her whole body stomping with freedom. Her eyes seem to relax from fear to welcome surprise, perhaps delight. I open the sliding glass door and call through the screen, "Well done. Well done." My family and I applaud.

As the day progresses, my thoughts return to the deer. While I prepare to teach my class, while Nyasha and I determine what we'll eat for dinner that evening, while I send the girls out to ride their bikes in the cul-de-sac, I think of the deer and wonder how she came to be stuck in our fence. I speculate that my wonder is rooted in my questions about how we perhaps have become stuck as well. *We* as in the broad we of society. How did we become stuck within a great multitude of fences—recent and extending into the distant past—unable to extricate ourselves from these constraints?

That night the girls ask if we can watch a show. As months have passed since this new existence first enclosed us, our regular consumption of *Family Matters* has diminished to occasional. Other activities have begun to occupy my time and thoughts. A return to my writing. My long-neglected knitting needles. My hand-lettering practice. My burgeoning interest in watercolors. And the girls have found other shows. Tonight, though, we stand around our kitchen island spooning pasta sauce over noodles. We fill glasses with ice water and grab the washcloths I bought years ago in lieu of cloth napkins, each of us reaching for our assigned color. In moments like these, life appears a replica of what has been and what could once again be. I find myself—momentarily—without expectation beyond food soon in my belly and a handful of hearty chuckles before bed. My mind finds rest from the thrum of questions about school returns and mask usage or when a pandemic might reach an end. And while the current reckoning with racism carries both hope and despair, tonight I allow myself to occupy a quieter space. Because there around the kitchen island, as we fill our dinner plates like we've always done, the troubles outside my home fade into the clouds. The chaos drifts away, leaving behind the fragile evening I have now.

"Let's watch *Family Matters*," I suggest. Like evenings past, everything we think will happen on the show does. Steve and Laura, Carl and Harriet, Eddie and Waldo, each displays the behavior we expect. I sink into the couch amid the girls' peals of laughter. Nyasha's smile catches the corner of my eye, and I lift a can of sparkling water to my lips. Outside, the sun sets and cars drive past our home. Night settles and streetlights turn to amber.

Anticipating Autumn

1.

The temperatures dipped last night, replacing the remnants of a tired summer with an autumn chill. The weather changed, and I shrugged on my first long-sleeved shirt of the season. Branches twitched against a subtle wind, and an overcast gray sky prophesied what the day might become. On this day, my younger daughter said from the back seat, "Mommy, are you going to die a long time from now? In forty years?" She asked this question with the casual acceptance that I will not be here forever and, for that matter, neither will she.

"I hope so," I replied. "I hope at least forty years."

The weather has changed, and I am beginning my fifth decade of life. Forty years from now, I will be eighty. If we live four seasons, perhaps I have taken a turn into my own autumn.

2.

Nyasha tells me the leaves may not turn this year. We journey to the mountains for our family's annual trek to an apple orchard. There we will wander dusty paths and pile crisp apples into baskets Nyasha pulls in a wagon. Over time, we've accumulated a series of annual photographs of the girls reaching their fingers into tree branches, emerging with giant smiles and ripe fruit.

"Our autumn has been too hot." Nyasha is summarizing a report he heard a few days back on public radio. He informs me that the leaves may skip the kaleidoscope of color and move straight to dead, the late heat robbing us of what we yearn to see.

In years past, we've driven these roads and relished the gentle rise and dip of hills set ablaze in vibrant reds and vivid oranges.

This year, though, I'm underwhelmed at a view still bright green with the past summer.

What is autumn, I wonder, in the absence of changing leaves?

3.

I find an altered form of me in the mirror. A plethora of silver strands streak my dark hair. *How did they become plentiful?* I think to myself and say to no one except the woman—both mysterious and utterly familiar—meeting my reflection in the glass. When I smile my full smile, mouth and eyes both, the prominence of crow's feet arrests me. I am, of course, an altered version of my past self. The insights the elapsed decades have brought adorn me like jewels placed in a crown. My body is aging, though. Lately, I ponder the fact that the time to use these insights shrinks as year collides into year.

A month before my fortieth birthday, I sat at the back of a hotel ballroom, taking notes as the speaker poured inspiration over the crowd. My pen rushed across the page, and my downturned eyes watched the formation of the slant of my cursive letters sprawling beyond my bulleted notes. When I looked at slides across the room, the letters and words blurred, everything a slight fog. For a nearly imperceptible moment, I inhabited that space of fuzzy becoming sharp. I struggled to see.

This past year, I spent the months before my actual birthday grafting myself—perhaps prematurely—into the spoils of my new decade. For that was how I saw it. Youth might disappear, but a certain hard-won contentment with life, I imagined that remaining. Shortly after I turned thirty-nine, I began telling people I was almost forty. Because I nearly was. In the timeline of my life, I might as well have been forty. The months rounded up to the multiple of ten. "My thirties were about finding liberation from meeting the expectations of others," I said to friends around a shared table. "I walk into this new decade feeling free." A great optimism seemed to engulf the words. The day I crossed that milestone birthday, I embraced the season of midlife.

4.

The weekend of my fortieth birthday, I dine at a rooftop restaurant with two of my oldest friends. They order cocktails, and I ask for a glass of blush wine. We order small plates to share. Chorizo-stuffed dates. Black truffle meatballs paired with fresh ricotta cheese. We wander to the balcony and pose for a series of pictures, our palms resting on our hips, elbows out, three old friends wearing matching black and white dresses. When we return to our seats, we continue the conversation we began in the car. "What's your biggest regret since graduation?"

We name old boyfriends. We speak of career choices and risks we should have taken. When we are together, time reverses to our nineteen-year-old selves. Without much thought, we assume the identities of our former lives. The years melt to nothing along with the heaviness and disenchantment the decades often bring. We all, together, remember who we were as we ate fries late at night at the O and squeezed into tube tops and skirts stopping just below our thighs. We stared at the future through a clear, shimmering lens of idealism, the world truly an oyster. Each of us destined to collect pearl after pearl after pearl.

We order another plate of chorizo-stuffed dates, and the manager appears with an apology. "The kitchen is out for the evening." The spicy, sweet taste we craved will be no more. He asks why we're all dressed alike. Zalenda points to me and says, "We're celebrating her birthday." Which can't quite explain the dresses my friends wore, nearly eleven years ago, at my wedding. But Zalenda's answer seems answer enough.

The manager jokes, "Twenty-six, right?"

"Plus fourteen," Sherae says, playing along.

"Twenty-six," he says again, his cheerful expression making us almost forget his news about the dates.

"No," I say. "Forty. Forty years old. I've earned every one of those years." Perhaps *earned* is not quite the word. But is there a specific word to encompass a belief that, past regrets or not, these have been good years?

5.

On a Saturday in mid-October, Nyasha texts me a photograph of our older daughter. Her arms rest on the top rail of a balcony. Her body turns toward the cityscape, the tall buildings behind, the rushing highway below. In the photograph, she is no longer the child who wraps her arms around me, hugs me tight, and states, "Mommy, I want to be stuck like glue to you." For a moment—a moment divided between reality and impossibility, between concrete and abstract—I can see the future. No, I can *feel* the future, as if the future might be a cozy blanket I can wrap around my shoulders or a mug of tea journeying down my throat. I feel the years ahead: the middle school years, where she will perhaps—officially—begin her path away from me, the high school years, where she'll dream of finding her own pearls, the college years, where she'll leave me the mother of a grown daughter. In that moment, what should lack clarity materializes as a vision drawn in distinct lines. Then reality pulls the comfort of my imaginations from me, and I am left with the picture of this girl, her face turned toward her father, who snapped the photograph. In my imagination, though, she turned her face toward me. When this future comes to fruition, when she settles into stadium seating in a college lecture hall, I will be transitioning into my next decade.

"Stuck like glue," my girl likes to tell me now. As if she can't imagine a day might come when she'll wander away from me, leaving me with empty arms that will reach for the ghost of a child now grown. I look through my girl's photographed eyes and sense the woman she is becoming. And perhaps this gauzy place of imagination enables me to envision the woman I am becoming, a woman planted in the midst, half a life behind me—before me, an unknown future.

6.

In mid-autumn I journey to a retreat center in the North Carolina mountains for a weeklong writing workshop. On the first truly cold day, a layer of fog rises above the hillside, a low cloud revealing the explosion of autumn leaves. Explosion. That's what one of the chefs tells me as I scrape up the remaining eggs on my plate. "It looked like it was going to be the worst leaf season ever," he tells me, even as we stare out the giant windows at the view, which proved that speculation and public radio wrong. He mentions how everything was just starting to go brown and then there was that one heavy rain. "It was just an explosion of color." By the time I walk back from the dining hall to my room, shivering in my light jacket, the morning sun has burned off the fog, and a blanket of light creeps up the hills. I am here for the best week autumn can offer, and there is no way I could have known that this might be. Even in the course of this week, I've watched sugar maples lose nearly all their leaves and the hillside lose its green. Part of me wants to guess at probabilities and possibilities, predictions and perfect timing. At the newly found age of forty, I walk down a trail cushioned in fallen leaves. It is clear—at least in my own mind—that all the glory, both the transience and permanence, all this was surely intended for me.

7.

Decades ago now, sawdust scattered at my father's feet. The subtle scent of burning wood and the shriek of an electric saw surrounded me. My outstretched palms had offered him my bit of driftwood bruised smooth by the ocean. That past summer, everyone else saw what was once a birch tree branch, but I saw a canoe in a found object's future. And from where I stood near my father's tool bench, removed from the sparks and grinding metal of the saw, I asked him to slice off the top length of the cylindrical shape and cut angles to create four edges. Later, as autumn cycled toward winter, I sat on the shaggy orange carpet in the family room. I spread newspaper on the floor to catch the wood crumbs. While we all watched television, I sanded my creation, turning the cut wood as smooth as the areas polished by waves. Then I took a chisel and hollowed out the cavity of my boat.

The year my father turned sixty, I was thirty, and my oldest daughter only a few months old. Sixty. Thirty. Zero. I remarked then at the pattern. From the vantage point of the middle, I could imagine myself like my daughter with a parent my age. I understood what my father once felt with a child my daughter's age. Ten years on, my daughter has reached her first decade, I am forty, and my father is a few months from seventy. Somewhere in the treasures I've preserved from my past years, a canoe carved from driftwood lies buried. Every now and again, I unearth this piece of wood. I show it to my daughters and think of my father. I remember a time that once was and is no more. The past becomes dust scattered at my feet.

8.

My mother stands behind where I sit, on a stool in her kitchen. She pats the back of my curls. The movement of her hand renders me a child seated on the red stool beneath the wall phone in the corner of a kitchen from long ago. My legs rest on the stool's steps, and my mother fries strips of bacon or browns mincemeat with onions at the stove close by. But I am not a child. Now her kitchen is absent the savory smells of breakfast meat or chopped onions sautéed in a pan. My hair twists away from my scalp, no longer secured in my youthful braids. "You really grew a lot of gray quickly," she says to me. She verbalizes what I've seen in the mirror, watching these thin lines appear within the ink of my hairline, glints of silver I once could count but now no more. I cannot see the back of my head. I cannot see what she sees. Her casual comment, though, seems to fill the air, present like a fog, refusing to dissipate, a certainty I've long suspected but never said.

My confession: I search strangers' hairlines for touches of silver. At a community discussion about finding home, I share much in common with the woman beside me. She sports a loose twist out and is also the child of Jamaican immigrants. For a season of life, we both lived in upstate New York. Her silver strands accent the sides of her hair, the same hue as mine. I place us both around a similar age.

I thought I might keep my dark hair for longer than average. I thought myself a special snowflake with the ability to push the silver strands aside and take enough deep breaths, take enough morning walks so stress wouldn't get to me. But in my mid-thirties what had once been a number I could count exploded in a way I almost thought my stylist had added streaks. Dark strands turned silver because of my parents, not because of stress. My father's arm hairs are nearly all white. My mother has a well-established head of much gray.

The stranger's silver strands spoke of solidarity in a season of life where our children are capable, our careers established. Our hair reflects the reality that the pigment cells in our follicles are dying. Each autumn, the leaves lose their color too, signs of their near end. My hair, a stranger's hair—in the changing, I know that one day I will crumple too.

9.

During my week in the mountains, on a trail walk, giant leaves of orange and red tap the ground. The sounds of living things chirp, whistle, and buzz nearby. Twigs crack, and I stumble upon the expanse of a graveyard. I spend ten minutes walking among the remains of the dead, stopping at tombstones and reading names of people I never knew existed and perhaps exist no more except in memory. Some grave markers bear recent dates—as close as three months prior. Other remains have rested here since before my birth. This must be a beautiful place to find oneself buried. These grave markers indicate lives lived until fifty, sixty, seventy, eighty, even ninety. My body will one day rest somewhere, somehow, perhaps in a cemetery where a gust of wind might loosen autumn leaves.

10.

Back in Charlotte, I wake to a day cast in gloom. No shards of light sneaking between dark clouds. No hints that the prognosis might turn. Raindrops vacillate between drizzle and pellets. Despite the conditions, I grab my umbrella and enter a world of low cloud coverage, wet pavement, and tire wheels splashing through puddles. I snap my umbrella open, hoisting it above my head, the changing leaves clinging to branches, some swaying through the air before landing on the ground. The scent of damp pavement mutes the slight odor of decaying vegetation, a hallmark of autumn.

In the coming months, I think I will dream once more. I will wake in the morning drowning in a pool of sunlight, and I will let the past fold in on itself. This is the beginning of my fifth decade of life. We are transient beings, stepping across earth for a finite amount of time. I won't weep over past mistakes. Instead, in the days and perhaps decades ahead, I will choose a tributary leading to new discoveries. I will declare with earnest gumption that each day, I can inhale afresh, I can try once more.

Now, though, in my neighborhood I walk familiar roads surrounded by trees dressed in mid-autumn. Amid a hundred fallen leaves, one beckons for me to stop mid-stride. Confined to its own block of pavement, the leaf rests face down, spider veins on full display. The edge lifts away from the ground, pale yellow, not having absorbed the moisture around. The body of the leaf, however, is darkening to near gold, soaked in the evidence of the morning wash. I fetch my phone from my pocket and capture this solitary leaf, both wet and dry, both pale and golden, in transition from life to death. Forty years from now—if I am here—perhaps I will have forgotten this moment and forgotten my awe. But I have experienced this moment now. Whatever may come tomorrow or reach forth across the years, today I stopped on this sidewalk. As my breathing pierced the membrane dividing present from future, I stared at this leaf. I noticed its placement on the wet ground. Surely my body and being will one day fade away. Before that time arrives, though, I can say with certainty that I have lived. I have lived. I have lived. Hoisting my umbrella again, I continue down the same path I walk most days.

By Way of Conclusion

To My Daughters—My Laughter and My Miracle,

That spring, a variety of colors seeped into the landscape. Yards gone to hay over the winter swiveled toward a whimpering green. For a few weeks, white dressed the dogwood beyond the fence. Then the flowers disappeared, replaced with a full, leafed-out covering. We talked of rabbits, bits of brown fur, still and silent in a patch of clover and then sprinting into the tall grass. And I resumed where I'd left off in the final days of autumn, when the dead leaves scattered beneath our maple tree. I returned to our front porch, phone in hand, now capturing buds breaking through branches. My commitments had shifted since the previous autumn, and I could no longer spend hours on the front porch. Despite the new patterns, I decided to freeze in time that nearly daily photograph. The maroon buds appeared and grew, day by day, until one day they expanded into delicate leaves no larger than the tip of my thumb. For a short while, the color of these fresh leaves reminded me more of autumn than spring. Perhaps the chlorophyll had yet to travel the plants' vein system to the perimeter of the leaves. Never before, though, not in springs past, had I noticed this slot of time more reminiscent of autumn's death than life. Of course, days passed and great leaves soon emerged as they always did.

That spring hopelessness had begun to swallow a house search we'd started the previous autumn. Houses beyond our budget. Houses others outbid us for. The churning days of waiting and longing, of clinging to bruised castles built in clouds. Then within a day, a seller accepted our offer. I turned my attention toward the boxes we needed to pack, toward the house we would soon leave and the one that would soon be ours. My mind drifted from the place we'd called home to the place we would make a home. Each day as I walked through the neighborhood that would soon be the place where you each began to swim or ride a tricycle, the place where you dressed as a pair of ladybugs for Halloween, the place where you celebrated birthdays and dug your fingers through the flatbed in the backyard, soon all this would become the place of our past lives and the people we once were. Your father purchased flattened boxes from the home improvement store. Each weekend, we taped those boxes together into containers to hold our lives. Stuffed animals. Framed photographs stripped from the wall. Boxes of books I labeled with permanent marker: Patrice's Office, Family Room, Spare Bedroom. Mementos and memories, objects and items stuffed away as if we could carry everything that might represent who we are.

That spring, as I took a walk through the neighborhood, conscious of inhaling the smells and remembering the sights of this place, I noticed a pack of vultures flying low to the ground, huddled together on the concrete. One leaned over, grasping a dead rabbit in its beak, and dragged the body along the sidewalk, a smear of burnt red trailing behind. I crossed the street, averting my eyes from the cruelty unfolding before me. That spring we waited for news about the trial of a white police officer who kneeled on George Floyd's neck. We learned of Daunte Wright, yet another black man whose life was snatched from him. That spring a white friend told me that she felt hopeful about the possibility of change. I read her text messages as I sat in lamplight, the spring darkness a comfort. Across the hallway, beyond the accumulating boxes, you both rested in a room slowly being undone. I thought of your drawings and stories packed away, your certificates, your books stacked near some of my childhood ones. The blooming of your lives fully in the season of spring. I reread my friend's words and wondered what it might be like to move through this world as she does, never experiencing what I experience. To be one who can so easily default to a position of hope—a word teeming with uncertainty of meaning, not offering a firm definition. At least in my mind.

You both slept across the hallway and stars sprinkled the night sky and I considered what I long for for you. How I want to ensure this world will treat you with kindness and celebrate wondrous you. How your father and I want to construct for you both a life that will allow your dreams to flourish, such that when you are in a class where you list your plans for the future, your desires for who you will become and what you will be, your list will fill pages, endless optimism that might steer you skyward with arms raised toward the clouds. Again and again, though, I am confronted with my inability to ensure these outcomes. I hope you will live lives incrementally better than mine. I hope a day will come void of racial violence and hierarchy. I hope for the promise of spring. And I believe I can give you the ability to find flecks of gold in murky water mixed in with pebbles and stones. I believe I can give you sight beyond eyesight that can seek out and find such treasures. Surely, I summon hope when I believe all this will come to pass.

That spring, one year to the day after George Floyd's murder, I participated in a conversation—ironically?—about hope. I sat at my desk, staring into the computer camera, my co-panelists scattered in other places. I spoke about hope with the heaviness of lack of hope dragging my temperament down. How difficult it was to converse as I recalled the past year and the past many years, the accumulation of racial violence mounting and mounting, a world that cries for a different way of being but cannot actually create it. "I want to burn it all down," I said that day to the other panelists. Flames reducing everything to nothing and perhaps letting us somehow start again. One panelist, with her wealth of knowledge about woods and trees and forests, said in those spaces, fires and flames can promote healing and growth.

That spring, I found myself, without fully realizing when or how it happened, crossing a threshold into another space. I would look at you both and know the season of young parenting was gliding away from me. The small humans you both are winking at the adults you will one day be. Yes, momentary conflicts or frustrations punctuated these days. Still, a relentless, satisfied sigh swept across the entirety of me as I bumped past either of you in the hallway. A contentment enclosed me as you both helped me prepare dinner, cutting yellow squash into cubes. As I sorted the framed photographs, glancing at moments from your past, I did not find my heart mingling with a yearning for years gone by. Instead, the contours of now and what might come became a pleasant shadow thrown across our lives.

That spring you packed up the dishes and pretend food in your play kitchen, long outgrown. We lugged everything over to the next-door neighbors, handing down the very thing we'd purchased used almost ten years before. You both planted tomato seeds and wild-flowers in the garden despite knowing our days in that home would soon be gone. You turned on the sprinkler and ran through the waving arcs of water as I once did, three decades ago, on my childhood lawn. These acts alone told me that life is not a linear trajectory and returns—perhaps in altered ways—again and again to itself.

That spring I discovered the very place I could locate tendrils of hope, the budding of what might be possible, the leaves the size of thumb tips that might grow into the length of my hand, is in the reality that while life circles in on itself, people can change. When seasons spiral back, actual seasons, spring and autumn, summer and winter, or seasons of life witnessed in future generations, we perhaps can no longer be the people we once were. The very fact that a human being can grow, I speculated this drew me closer to hope. Like so many others in our world, each season that passes, I change, your father changes, you both change as well.

That spring became that summer, and we moved into our new home. We unpacked the boxes, arranged the furniture, rolled out new rugs. We determined which cupboards would hold the glasses and mugs, which drawers the silverware. I stashed art supplies in various corners of the house, a desk drawer here, a rolling cart there, a basket on a bookshelf. I organized my new office, turned my desk toward the window, framed several of your drawings for display on the wall. That summer became that autumn, and I turned my eyes toward what grew within our home rather than what grew beyond. I sat and stared for stretches of time at the plants I'd purchased and potted, displayed on the mantle above the fireplace, the dining room table, and the corner of my desk. Bits of green expanding to sprout new leaves after I thought I couldn't nurture a plant through the first few weeks. Ficus leaves. Aloe spears. Nameless succulents turning from red to yellow. Instead of time spent observing the changing maple tree, I watched my community of house plants drinking the sun near each window. Leaves and stems exhaling oxygen. I told you girls that I'd read that I am now a plant mom, concerned with the health of these living things. Your grandmother gave me clippings from a fern she first nurtured years before my birth. I grasped a belief—tightly grasped—that this legacy would take to new soil. And, in a few months' time, I would repot *my* fern in a more permanent home.

That autumn I looked back on the past spring and remembered how my maple tree photographs petered out once I no longer noticed any change. I recalled how my gaze shifted to the logistics of moving, and I forgot to stare. Only in the final days we lived in that house did I think, really think of how I would not spend another autumn connected to the life of that tree. There would not be another spring. I remembered how you both would shimmy high into the branches, and I'd suppress my desire to say, "Be careful." To my own surprise, I found myself wanting to weep for both the tree that I would no longer watch and a time of life that has faded. Nostalgia's fingers seemed to gently rap at our front door. Even more, though, I mourned my inattentiveness to the reality of life that had shifted without my observation or notation.

I sit now writing these words, remembering both spring's contentment with change and autumn's sorrow because of change. These seeming contradictions, in fact, are merely multiple facets of the ongoing engagement with our unfolding days. So, I say to both of you, may you walk each season with hands open, breathing in the truth of the past and the possibility of what might come, all the while touching what is tangible and concrete about now. Perhaps tomorrow or next week will invite you to further complicate your view of yourself, the world, or those around you. Whether or not that happens, what is certain is this lifetime already has and this lifetime always will.

That autumn there was a Sunday afternoon in our new home, a day where I would spend hours on our couch tangled up in my books. A time came that day when you girls and your father prepared lunch in the kitchen. I heard your father tell a story from his childhood, one we all know but I can't recall now. Your laughter and questions added commentary, the storytelling more of a ritual than a conveyor of information or entertainment. My eyes moved from the make-believe characters on the page to the living people in front of me. With conscious effort, I let that moment etch a pattern into my brain. The vision of your faces and the sound of smiles woven into your speech. You all finished stacking together sandwiches and exited the kitchen. When I returned to my book, the words drew me in once more. Tucked around the periphery of thought, a static sketch of lives in motion—dare I say transformation—joined my memory folds.

With love always,
Your Mama

GRATITUDE

First, thank you to you, dear reader, for choosing to spend time with these words. In a world with much that competes for our attention, the choice to open one particular book is no small thing. I am grateful for your interest. And if you loved these essays, please tell someone else and leave a review on Goodreads, etc.

Thank you to the editors who previously published some of these essays. Your early interest in this work helped shape what this book has become.

Thank you to the Charlotte Mecklenburg Library. Your assistance as I conducted research for several of the essays was invaluable. I'm grateful for your responses to my questions, your searches through materials, your desire to help.

Thank you to Courtney Ochsner, Kayla Moslander, Rosemary Sekora, Tish Fobben, Lindsey Welch, Jackson Adams, Leif Milliken, and the entire team at the University of Nebraska Press. It has been such a joy working with you. The energy and excitement, care and compassion you have for this work affirm again and again that UNP is the perfect home for these words. Thank you to Stephanie Ward. Your editorial input made *Autumn Song* even stronger. Your words of praise are a lasting encouragement.

Thank you to the North Carolina Arts Council, the Arts & Science Council of Charlotte Mecklenburg County, and the Collegeville Institute for the generous support that helped make space for me to create some of the work in this book.

Thank you to the many who took the time to read early drafts of these essays. Your feedback, insights, and encouragement leave fingerprints. Yes, we may create alone, but we also create together.

Thank you to Roohi Choudhry, Kate Motaung, Lisa Ohlen Harris, and Denise Flanders. Your boundless support as this manuscript journeyed from my computer to perfect publication home will stay with me always. It is an incredible gift to have such people in my life.

To my daughters, thank you for being your wildly creative, imaginative, and self-starting selves. Who you are enables your mother to be the writer she is. And Nyasha, thank you for showering me with a steady love that challenges me and inspires me and buoys me to believe that my hopes and dreams will, of course, come to fruition. You always see a stunning future.

Finally, thank you always to the One who calls and is faithful to do it. Thank you for sacred whispers of what could be.

SOURCE ACKNOWLEDGMENTS

The following essays were previously published, sometimes in a different form:

"Blueberry Season": *Full Grown People*, June 21, 2018.

"Winter's Breakup": *Lunch Ticket—Amuse Bouche*, January 2016.

"That Autumn": *Charlotte Magazine*, August 2019. It won a City and Regional Magazine Award for best essay/commentary/criticism. It was also a Notable Essay in *The Best American Essays 2020*.

"Between Mountains and Water": as "North Star" in AFAR *Magazine*, September/October 2021.

"Raised to Life": *The Journal of Compressed Creative Arts*, November 2016.

"I Think My Grandmother Has Forgotten": *Brain, Child Magazine* (online), January 2016.

"A Moment Leads to an Essay": *CharlotteLit* blog, December 3, 2018.

"More Than Tea": *Paper & String*, April 2020.

A portion of "The Blooming of Mournful Things": as "A Doll Like Me" in *The Brevity Podcast*, no. 10 (September 2018).

A portion of "The Blooming of Mournful Things": as "Something a Little Different" in *Beautiful Truth: A Gathering of Voices from Charlotte*, NC, 2019.

A portion of "The Blooming of Mournful Things": as "A Voice Not Heard" in *Thread* 4, no.1 (Spring 2018).

A portion of "The Blooming of Mournful Things": as part of "Four from the Night, Four from Anywhere" in *The Mudroom*, June 2018.

A portion of "The Blooming of Mournful Things": as "Wild-flowers" in *River Teeth*'s Beautiful Things column, September 2014.

"What Is Common, What Is Rare": *Catapult*, January 14, 2019.

"Our Words at a Moment in Time": *Brevity* blog, February 21, 2018.

"Two Field Guides": *Full Grown People*, December 10, 2015.

AUTHOR COMMENTS

That Autumn

With regards to this essay and subsequent essays, one area that bears mentioning concerns my lowercase spelling of *black* in reference to a race of people. In my first book of essays, I explained my reasons for not capitalizing *black*. I wrote, "I do believe that in this country being black is to embrace both a race and an ethnicity, so I wonder if I meet the qualifications for being *Black*. Do I fit the standards that allow me full acceptance in that group?" I considered my Jamaican ancestry, my multiracial heritage, my experience with other black Americans questioning my blackness, and I pondered, "Does my experience align well enough to live with a capitalized *B*?" I concluded, "By choosing to use the lowercase *b*, I am saying that I want to be included in this definition. I want the word to be expansive enough to draw me within the curves and twists of the letters."

However, during the summer of 2020, as protests for racial justice reached across the country and around the world, I returned to this idea of the capital *B*. Whereas once I had questioned if the capital *B* was large enough to include me, I recognized my developing doubts about my previous position. Perhaps the capital *B* now felt wide and welcoming. Perhaps I had changed. Perhaps society had changed as well. In this collection, I continue to use the lowercase *b*. With the older essays, this choice reflects my past position. With the new essays, though, the lowercase *b* instead serves to create consistency across the essays. Please know, though, that behind the lowercase *b* resides someone who once thought the capital *B* not large enough to include her. I am now a writer reconsidering, as we are all wont to do in life. The use of this lowercase *b* preserves a moment in time of who I was. In this note, though, my discussion of the topic points to where my thinking is leading me. In my next book of essays, I suspect readers will find the capital version of the letter. We live our lives with space to embrace the possibility of changing our minds.

I Think My Grandmother Has Forgotten

In the final days of 2020, at the age of ninety-four, my grandmother on my father's side passed away. That morning, my brother-in-law said, "Only a worldwide pandemic and apocalyptic conditions could take out Grandma." That night Nyasha, the girls, and I ate Sara Lee pound cake, one of the few sweets my grandmother was prone to eat. Before we partook of the treat, we each shared adjectives describing her. Courageous. Competitive. Fun and Funny. Hardworking. The horrible thing about dementia is the way it seeks to snatch the memory of the person you love. At the front of your mind are the recent memories of the person struggling to remember. The space I want to exist in, though, even as I treasure this essay, is the space of remembering who my grandmother was across her life and across my life. My grandmother said it like it was and often made decisions based solely on her opinion. If she didn't like the flowers growing alongside our home, she'd pull them up. If she thought you didn't shine in an outfit, she'd surely tell you. She'd challenge people to a race and inquire if they could touch their toes before leaning to reach for her feet. She always wanted to be early wherever she went and she collected small objects from her travels and she wore hats to church. She loved me, she loved me, she loved me, and she believed I was capable of anything. I write these details as if a few sentences could capture my grandmother's life—even as I know I've failed to do her justice in the essays that mention her in this book. What I thought the morning of her death, though, is she lived life with boldness and courage and lack of fear about what others might think of her. She said what she wanted to say, using her voice, not defaulting to a place of censoring herself. These qualities helped my grandmother build a life that would serve as beginnings for her children, her grandchildren, her great-grandchildren.

Two Field Guides

There is much I still admire about this essay, but I also think, in a way, the narrator has a youthful naivety I find myself no longer as ready to muster. Perhaps this is a clear example of an essay where the narrator is now absent. At the time of writing, I believe I infused this piece with a great deal of nuance about the challenges that may creep into friendships like the one presented in the essay. However, one area I now realize I failed to consider is the reality of power imbalances. Friendships should be egalitarian in nature. Power imbalances as a result of society's broken race relations have a detrimental impact on individual relationships. To that end, if I were to write this essay again, I would work harder to tease out blame and responsibility rather than equally placing it at the feet of both. Yes, both friends bear some level of responsibility, but how much and what are not the same for the black person and the white person. That recognition matters in ongoing discussions about race and interpersonal relationships. If I were to rewrite the ending, I would now emphasize further the ongoing nature of choosing to connect across the vast brokenness created by a fractured society and lived out by individuals. Reaching a point of reconciliation is no guarantee that challenges won't surface again in the future. As people live, they experience growth in their understanding of the multitude of ways power and injustice impact friendships. Friends can once again find themselves in those rocky waters of confusion, frustration, and discontent.

Power imbalances because of historic hierarchy impact conflict. Awareness can influence if or how these conflicts resolve. For what it's worth, though, I believe this essay captures well the possible struggles and gifts these types of friendships can experience when they delve into the realm of the uncomfortable.

My Pandemic Days: March–July 2020

Of all the essays in this book, "My Pandemic Days" varies most from what I might write now if I took the opportunity to begin once more. The pandemic brought a time of constant motion and movement and change—both in the external world and in my internal processing of what I saw, heard, remembered, and experienced. As I alluded to within the actual essay, the words became seemingly outdated before I could turn my handwritten scribbles into typed pages. What was the use of my attempts to document those first four months? Why bother to seek to make sense of the angle from which I lived through a global happening and reckoning? However, I look back on these words as preserving a time of extreme vulnerability and uncertainty, capturing this moment for future examination. Those four months were the beginning of the beginning moving toward the end of the beginning and the beginning of the middle. That was a time when the average individual was only starting to grasp the distance to the beginning of the end and perhaps not quite to the point of wondering if the end of the end would ever or could ever arrive. My story is but one tiny lens examining the sliver of the world I occupied at that time. I hope as time continues forward, there will be an abundance of tiny lenses shared from all walks of life. Only in this way can we, as a society, piece together the reality of this global tragedy affecting some individuals and communities, some cities and countries far more than others.

By Way of Conclusion

In this essay, I write, "When seasons spiral back, actual seasons, spring and autumn, summer and winter, or seasons of life witnessed in future generations, we perhaps can no longer be the people we once were." These words arrived from a meditative posture I had taken while writing this essay and assembling this collection. The concept that life is a spiral and not a straight line drifted in and out of my thinking. My first conscious encounter with this concept occurred as I read *Falling Upward: A Spirituality for the Two Halves of Life* by Fr. Richard Rohr. I add the word *conscious* because these ideas are often floating around us, only sticking to our minds when the time comes for them to matter. I read *Falling Upward* while seated on my front porch during the early months of a global pandemic. Over time, I've realized that the concept of life being a spiral and not a straight line is not original to Rohr. However, reflecting on those words through that first pandemic spring altered my engagement with the following months, and now years. For that, I am grateful.

NOTES

That Autumn

1. Clint Smith and Jelani Cobb, "The Desegregation and Resegregation of Charlotte's Schools," *New Yorker*, October 3, 2016, https://www.newyorker.com/news/news-desk/the-desegregation-and-resegregation-of-charlottes-schools.

2. Alana Semuels, "Why It's So Hard to Get Ahead in the South," *The Atlantic*, April 6, 2017, https://www.theatlantic.com/business/archive/2017/04/south-mobility-charlotte/521763/.

3. Thomas W. Hanchett, "Creating Black Neighborhoods," in *Sorting out the New South City: Race, Class, and Urban Development in Charlotte, 1875–1975*, by Thomas W. Hanchett (Chapel Hill: The University of North Carolina Press, 1998), 130–34.

4. Hanchett, "Creating Black Neighborhoods," 130–34.

5. Bill Arthur, "Business Booms Where a Slum Once Festered," *Charlotte Observer*, May 20, 1973, C1, C5.

6. Joe Doster, "Slum Razing Project Approved by Council," *Charlotte Observer*, January 19, 1960, A1–A2.

7. Redevelopment Commission of the City of Charlotte, "Urban Renewal in Charlotte: The First Five Years (Annual Report)," 1963.

8. Sheila Vance, "Brooklyn: Lost Community Lives Again in Memories," *Charlotte News*, July 18, 1977, B4, B14; Curtina Perkins Simmons, "People Made Brooklyn Special," *Mecklenburg Neighbors*, February 21, 1988; Milton Jordan, "A Story of Renewal in Brooklyn," *Charlotte Observer*, June 5, 1977, C1, C4.

9. Ta-Nehisi Coates, "The Case for Reparations," *The Atlantic*, May 14, 2014, https://www.theatlantic.com/magazine/archive/2014/06/the-case-for-reparations/361631/.

10. Coates, "The Case for Reparations."

11. Arthur, "Business Booms," C1, C5.

12. Semuels, "Why It's So Hard to Get Ahead."

13. Vivian Ross Nivens, "'I Sure Loved It . . . Cause It Was Home,'" *Charlotte Observer*, May 20, 1973, C4.

14. Arthur, "Business Booms," C1, C5.

15. Jordan, "A Story of Renewal in Brooklyn."

16. Arthur, "Business Booms," C1, C5.

Stones of Remembrance

1. Brian Handwerk, "Leap Year Saved Our Societies from Chaos—For Now, at Least," *National Geographic*, February 21, 2020, https://www.nationalgeographic.com/science/article/160226-leap-year-science-time-world-cultures-february.

2. Handwerk, "Leap Year Saved Our Societies."

3. Mary Bellis, "Who Invented Leap Year?" ThoughtCo, accessed August 14, 2021, https://www.thoughtco.com/history-of-leap-year-1989846.

When the *Challenger* Exploded

1. Sarah Pruitt, "5 Things You May Not Know about the Challenger Shuttle Disaster," History.com, A&E Television Networks, January 28, 2016, https://www.history.com/news/5-things-you-might-not-know-about-the-challenger-shuttle-disaster; History.com Editors, "Challenger Explosion," History.com, A&E Television Networks, February 15, 2010, https://www.history.com/topics/1980s/challenger-disaster.

2. Lee Margulies, "Episode to Air March 9: 'Punky' Deals with Shuttle Tragedy," *Los Angeles Times*, February 19, 1986, https://www.latimes.com/archives/la-xpm-1986-02-19-ca-9722-story.html.

3. John C. Wright et al., "How Children Reacted to Televised Coverage of the Space Shuttle Disaster," *Journal of Communication* 39, no. 2 (January 1989): 27–45, https://doi.org/10.1111/j.1460-2466.1989.tb01027.x.

4. Denise Lineberry, "To Sleep or Not to Sleep?" NASA, April 14, 2009, https://www.nasa.gov/centers/langley/news/researchernews/rn_sleep.html.

5. Pruitt, "5 Things You May Not Know."

6. Pruitt, "5 Things You May Not Know."

7. Kalhan Rosenblatt, "5.1 Magnitude Earthquake Hits North Carolina, Most Powerful in the State since 1916," NBCNews.com, NBC Universal News Group, August 9, 2020, https://www.nbcnews.com/news/us-news/5-1-magnitude-earthquake-hits-north-carolina-most-powerful-state-n1236238.

A Moment Leads to an Essay

1. "Musa Balbisiana COLLA: Plants of the World Online: Kew Science," Plants of the World Online, Royal Botanic Gardens, Kew, accessed August 13, 2021, http://www.plantsoftheworldonline.org/taxon/urn:lsid:ipni.org: names:797536-1; Jesse Rhodes, "Taming the Wild Banana," Smithsonian .com, July 21, 2011, https://www.smithsonianmag.com/arts-culture/taming -the-wild-banana-33985103/.

And There Will Be Gifts

1. *The Golden Hands Complete Book of Knitting & Crochet* (New York: Random House, 1973), 14.
2. *The Golden Hands Complete Book of Knitting & Crochet* (New York: Random House, 1973), 35.
3. *The Golden Hands Complete Book of Knitting & Crochet* (New York: Random House, 1973), 15.

A Brief Statement on Grace

1. E. S. C. Weiner and J. A. Simpson, "Grace," in *The Oxford English Dictionary* (Oxford: Clarendon Press, 1989), 718–721; "Grace," Online Etymology Dictionary, accessed August 12, 2021, https://www.etymonline.com/word /grace.

Single-Family Zoning Considered

1. "Fastest-Growing Cities Primarily in the South and West," The United States Census Bureau, August 17, 2020, https://www.census.gov/newsroom /press-releases/2019/subcounty-population-estimates.html.
2. Steve Harrison, "Charlotte City Council Members Balk at Push to Eliminate SINGLE-FAMILY ZONING," WFAE 90.7—Charlotte's NPR News Source, May 7, 2021, https://www.wfae.org/2021-03-03/city-council -members-balk-at-push-to-eliminate-single-family-only-zoning.
3. Harrison, "Charlotte City Council Members Balk."
4. Eric Jaffe, "Is It Time to End Single-Family Zoning?" Sidewalk Talk, Medium, February 6, 2020, https://medium.com/sidewalk-talk/is-it -time-to-end-single-family-zoning-56233d69a25a.
5. Emily Badger and Quoctrung Bui, "Cities Start to Question an American Ideal: A House with a Yard on Every Lot," *New York Times,* June 18, 2019, https://www.nytimes.com/interactive/2019/06/18/upshot/cities-across -america-question-single-family-zoning.html.

6. Erin Baldassari and Molly Solomon, "The Racist History of Single-Family Home Zoning," KQED, October 5, 2020, https://www.kqed.org/news /11840548/the-racist-history-of-single-family-home-zoning.

7. *Charlotte Future, 2040 Comprehensive Plan, Public Review Draft 2020*, 1–320.

8. *Charlotte Future, 2040 Comprehensive Plan, Public Review Draft 2020*, 42.

9. Julie Rose, "Racist Clauses Plague Property Deeds in Charlotte, across Country," WFAE 90.7—Charlotte's NPR News Source, September 27, 2012, https://www.wfae.org/local-news/2010-01-11/racist-clauses-plague -property-deeds-in-charlotte-across-country; "Home Ownership and the Legacy of Redlining," UNC Charlotte Urban Institute, May 18, 2020, https://ui.uncc.edu/story/home-ownership-and-legacy-redlining.

10. Hunter Sáenz, "Charlotte Could Eliminate Single-Family Only ZONING: What It Means for Your Neighborhood," wcnc.com, March 2, 2021, https:// www.wcnc.com/article/money/markets/real-estate/charlotte-single -family-zoning-ordinance/275-71e61941-2e39-4f0e-9235-8b3c2d0a903e.

11. Sáenz, "Charlotte Could Eliminate Single-Family Only ZONING."

12. *Charlotte Future, 2040 Comprehensive Plan, Public Review Draft 2020*, 10.

13. Chuck Bryant and Josh Clark, "How Housing Discrimination Works," accessed August 11, 2021, https://podcasts.apple.com/us/podcast/stuff -you-should-know/id278981407?i=1000508582300.

14. Jung Hyun Choi, "Breaking down the Black-White Homeownership Gap," Urban Institute, February 21, 2020, https://www.urban.org/urban-wire /breaking-down-black-white-homeownership-gap.

15. Ta-Nehisi Coates, "The Case for Reparations," *The Atlantic*, May 14, 2014, https://www.theatlantic.com/magazine/archive/2014/06/the-case-for -reparations/361631/.

16. Adrian Higgins, "Scientists Thought They Had Created the Perfect Tree. But It Became a Nightmare," *Washington Post*, September 27, 2018, https://www.washingtonpost.com/lifestyle/magazine/how-we-turned -the-bradford-pear-into-a-monster/2018/09/14/f29c8f68-91b6-11e8 -b769-e3fff17f0689_story.html.

17. "Charlotte Metro Area Population 1950–2021," MacroTrends, accessed August 11, 2021, https://www.macrotrends.net/cities/22954/charlotte /population.

18. Paul Davidson, "Black Households Can Afford Just 25% of Homes for Sale, down from 39% in 2012," *USA Today*, October 15, 2019, https://www .usatoday.com/story/money/2019/10/15/homes-sale-black-households -can-afford-just-25-percent-houses-market/3976383002/.

19. Tommy Tomlinson, "Charlotte Is 250 Years Old. What Will We Look like after 250 More?" WFAE 90.7—Charlotte's NPR News Source, December 4, 2018, https://www.wfae.org/commentaries/2018-12-03/charlotte-is -250-years-old-what-will-we-look-like-after-250-more.

What Is Common, What Is Rare

1. Marcia Dunn, "Total Solar Eclipse 1st in 99 Years to Sweep Width of US," AP NEWS, June 23, 2017, https://apnews.com/article/north-america-ia -state-wire-id-state-wire-oregon-charleston-22086fc5072b44f9a6574dc 7e549cccd.

2. Patrice Gopo, *All the Colors We Will See: Reflections on Barriers, Brokenness, and Finding Our Way* (Nashville TN: W. Publishing Group, an imprint of Thomas Nelson, 2018), 198.

My Pandemic Days

1. Rob Picheta, "People in India Can See the Himalayas for the First Time In 'Decades,' as the Lockdown EASES Air Pollution," CNN, April 9, 2020, https://www.cnn.com/travel/article/himalayas-visible-lockdown-india -scli-intl/index.html.

2. Julia Jacobo, "Venice Canals Are Clear Enough to See Fish as Coronavirus Halts Tourism in the City," ABC News, March 18, 2020, https://abcnews .go.com/International/venice-canals-clear-fish-coronavirus-halts-tourism -city/story?id=69662690.

3. "Coronavirus: Lions Nap on Road during South African Lockdown," BBC News, April 16, 2020, https://www.bbc.com/news/world-africa -52314282.

4. Marc Martin, "These Stunning Photos Show Yosemite without Humans. Animals Are Taking Over," *Los Angeles Times*, April 13, 2020, https://www .latimes.com/california/story/2020-04-13/coronavirus-closure-returns -yosemite-to-the-animals.

BIBLIOGRAPHY

Arthur, Bill. "Business Booms Where a Slum Once Festered." *Charlotte Observer*, May 20, 1973.

Badger, Emily, and Quoctrung Bui. "Cities Start to Question an American Ideal: A House with a Yard on Every Lot." *New York Times*, June 18, 2019. https://www.nytimes.com/interactive/2019/06/18/upshot/cities-across-america-question-single-family-zoning.html.

Baldassari, Erin, and Molly Solomon. "The Racist History of Single-Family Home Zoning." KQED. October 5, 2020. https://www.kqed.org/news/11840548/the-racist-history-of-single-family-home-zoning.

Bellis, Mary. "Who Invented Leap Year?" ThoughtCo. Accessed August 14, 2021. https://www.thoughtco.com/history-of-leap-year-1989846.

Bryant, Chuck, and Josh Clark. "How Housing Discrimination Works." *Stuff You Should Know*, February 11, 2021. Podcast, 54:14. https://podcasts.apple.com/us/podcast/stuff-you-should-know/id278981407?i=1000508582300.

"Challenger Explosion." History.com. A&E Television Networks. February 15, 2010. https://www.history.com/topics/1980s/challenger-disaster.

"Charlotte Metro Area Population 1950–2021." MacroTrends. Accessed August 11, 2021. https://www.macrotrends.net/cities/22954/charlotte/population.

Choi, Jung Hyun. "Breaking down the Black-White Homeownership Gap." Urban Institute. February 21, 2020. https://www.urban.org/urban-wire/breaking-down-black-white-homeownership-gap.

City of Charlotte, *Charlotte Future, 2040 Comprehensive Plan, Public Review Draft 2020.*

Coates, Ta-Nehisi. "The Case for Reparations." *The Atlantic*, May 14, 2014. https://www.theatlantic.com/magazine/archive/2014/06/the-case-for-reparations/361631/.

"Coronavirus: Lions Nap on Road during South African Lockdown." BBC News. April 16, 2020. https://www.bbc.com/news/world-africa-52314282.

Davidson, Paul. "Black Households Can Afford Just 25% of Homes for Sale, down from 39% in 2012." *USA Today*, October 15, 2019. https://www

.usatoday.com/story/money/2019/10/15/homes-sale-black-households
-can-afford-just-25-percent-houses-market/3976383002/.

Doster, Joe. "Slum Razing Project Approved by Council." *Charlotte Observer*,
January 19, 1960.

Dunn, Marcia. "Total Solar Eclipse 1st in 99 Years to Sweep Width of US." AP
NEWS. June 23, 2017. https://apnews.com/article/north-america-ia-state
-wire-id-state-wire-oregon-charleston-22086fc5072b44f9a6574dc7e54
9cccd.

"Fastest-Growing Cities Primarily in the South and West." The United States
Census Bureau. August 17, 2020. https://www.census.gov/newsroom/press
-releases/2019/subcounty-population-estimates.html.

The Golden Hands Complete Book of Knitting & Crochet. New York: Random
House, 1973.

Gopo, Patrice. *All the Colors We Will See: Reflections on Barriers, Brokenness,
and Finding Our Way*. Nashville TN: W. Publishing Group, an imprint of
Thomas Nelson, 2018.

"Grace." Online Etymology Dictionary. Accessed August 12, 2021. https://
www.etymonline.com/word/grace.

Hanchett, Thomas W. "Creating Black Neighborhoods." In *Sorting out the
New South City: Race, Class, and Urban Development in Charlotte, 1875–1975*,
by Thomas W. Hanchett, 130–34. Chapel Hill: The University of North
Carolina Press, 1998.

Handwerk, Brian. "Leap Year Saved Our Societies from Chaos—For Now,
at Least." *National Geographic*, February 21, 2020. https://www.national
geographic.com/science/article/160226-leap-year-science-time-world
-cultures-february.

Harrison, Steve. "Charlotte City Council Members Balk at Push to Eliminate
Single-Family Zoning." WFAE 90.7—Charlotte's NPR News Source. May
7, 2021. https://www.wfae.org/2021-03-03/city-council-members-balk
-at-push-to-eliminate-single-family-only-zoning.

Higgins, Adrian. "Scientists Thought They Had Created the Perfect Tree. But
It Became a Nightmare." *Washington Post*, September 27, 2018. https://www
.washingtonpost.com/lifestyle/magazine/how-we-turned-the-bradford
-pear-into-a-monster/2018/09/14/f29c8f68-91b6-11e8-b769-e3fff17f0689
_story.html.

History.com Editors. "Challenger Explosion." History.com. A&E Television
Networks. February 15, 2010. https://www.history.com/topics/1980s
/challenger-disaster.

"Home Ownership and the Legacy of Redlining." UNC Charlotte Urban Institute. May 18, 2020. https://ui.uncc.edu/story/home-ownership-and-legacy-redlining.

Jacobo, Julia. "Venice Canals Are Clear Enough to See Fish as Coronavirus Halts Tourism in the City." ABC News. March 18, 2020. https://abcnews.go.com/International/venice-canals-clear-fish-coronavirus-halts-tourism-city/story?id=69662690.

Jaffe, Eric. "Is It Time to End Single-Family Zoning?" Sidewalk Talk. Medium. February 6, 2020. https://medium.com/sidewalk-talk/is-it-time-to-end-single-family-zoning-56233d69a25a.

Lineberry, Denise. "To Sleep or Not to Sleep?" NASA. April 14, 2009. https://www.nasa.gov/centers/langley/news/researchernews/rn_sleep.html.

Margulies, Lee. "Episode to Air March 9: 'Punky' Deals with Shuttle Tragedy." *Los Angeles Times*, February 19, 1986. https://www.latimes.com/archives/la-xpm-1986-02-19-ca-9722-story.html.

Martin, Marc. "These Stunning Photos Show Yosemite without Humans. Animals Are Taking Over." *Los Angeles Times*, April 13, 2020. https://www.latimes.com/california/story/2020-04-13/coronavirus-closure-returns-yosemite-to-the-animals.

"Musa Balbisiana COLLA: Plants of the World Online: Kew Science." Plants of the World Online. Royal Botanic Gardens, Kew. Accessed August 13, 2021. http://www.plantsoftheworldonline.org/taxon/urn:lsid:ipni.org:names:797536-1.

Perkins Simmons, Curtina. "People Made Brooklyn Special." *Mecklenburg Neighbors*, February 21, 1988.

Picheta, Rob. "People in India Can See the Himalayas for the First Time In 'Decades,' as the Lockdown Eases Air Pollution." CNN. April 9, 2020. https://www.cnn.com/travel/article/himalayas-visible-lockdown-india-scli-intl/index.html.

Pruitt, Sarah. "5 Things You May Not Know about the Challenger Shuttle Disaster." History.com. A&E Television Networks. January 28, 2016. https://www.history.com/news/5-things-you-might-not-know-about-the-challenger-shuttle-disaster.

Redevelopment Commission of the City of Charlotte. *Urban Renewal in Charlotte: The First Five Years (Annual Report)*. 1963.

Rhodes, Jesse. "Taming the Wild Banana." Smithsonian.com. July 21, 2011. https://www.smithsonianmag.com/arts-culture/taming-the-wild-banana-33985103/.

Rose, Julie. "Racist Clauses Plague Property Deeds in Charlotte, across Country." WFAE 90.7—Charlotte's NPR News Source. September 27, 2012. https://www.wfae.org/local-news/2010-01-11/racist-clauses-plague -property-deeds-in-charlotte-across-country.

Rosenblatt, Kalhan. "5.1 Magnitude Earthquake Hits North Carolina, Most Powerful in the State since 1916." NBCNews.com. NBC Universal News Group. August 9, 2020. https://www.nbcnews.com/news/us-news/5-1 -magnitude-earthquake-hits-north-carolina-most-powerful-state-n123 6238.

Ross Nivens, Vivian. "'I Sure Loved It . . . Cause It Was Home.'" *Charlotte Observer*, May 20, 1973.

Sáenz, Hunter. "Charlotte Could Eliminate Single-Family Only Zoning: What It Means for Your Neighborhood." wcnc.com. March 2, 2021. https://www .wcnc.com/article/money/markets/real-estate/charlotte-single-family -zoning-ordinance/275-71e61941-2e39-4f0e-9235-8b3c2d0a903e.

Semuels, Alana. "Why It's So Hard to Get Ahead in the South." *The Atlantic*, April 6, 2017. https://www.theatlantic.com/business/archive/2017/04 /south-mobility-charlotte/521763/.

Smith, Clint, and Jelani Cobb. "The Desegregation and Resegregation of Charlotte's Schools." *New Yorker*, October 3, 2016. https://www.newyorker .com/news/news-desk/the-desegregation-and-resegregation-of-charlottes -schools.

Tomlinson, Tommy. "Charlotte Is 250 Years Old. What Will We Look Like after 250 More?" WFAE 90.7—Charlotte's NPR News Source. December 4, 2018. https://www.wfae.org/commentaries/2018-12-03/charlotte-is -250-years-old-what-will-we-look-like-after-250-more.

Tutu, Desmond. "10 Pieces of Wisdom from Desmond Tutu on His Birth-day." Desmond Tutu Foundation USA. October 21, 2015. http://www .tutufoundationusa.org/2015/10/07/10-pieces-of-wisdom-from-desmond -tutu-on-his-birthday/.

Vance, Sheila. "Brooklyn: Lost Community Lives Again in Memories." *Charlotte News*, July 18, 1977.

Weiner, E. S. C., and J. A. Simpson. "Grace." In *The Oxford English Dictionary*, 718–21. Oxford: Clarendon Press, 1989.

Wright, John C., Dale Kunkel, Marites Pinon, and Aletha C. Huston. "How Children Reacted to Televised Coverage of the Space Shuttle Disaster." *Journal of Communication* 39, no. 2 (1989): 27–45. https://doi.org/10.1111 /j.1460-2466.1989.tb01027.x.

IN THE AMERICAN LIVES SERIES

To order or obtain more information on these or other University of Nebraska Press titles, visit nebraskapress.unl.edu.

Printed in the USA
CPSIA information can be obtained
at www.ICGtesting.com
LVHW091223151223
766489LV00004B/401